Smoky Jack

Smoky Jack

The Adventures of a Dog and His Master on Mount Le Conte

By Paul J. Adams
Edited by Anne Bridges and Ken Wise

THE UNIVERSITY OF TENNESSEE PRESS
Knoxville

Library of Congress Cataloging-in-Publication Data

Names: Adams, Paul J. (Paul Jay), author.
Title: Smoky Jack : the adventures of a dog and his master on Mount Le Conte /
by Paul J. Adams ; Anne Bridges and Ken Wise, editors.
Description: First edition. | Knoxville : The University of Tennessee Press, 2016.
| Includes bibliographical references.
Identifiers: LCCN 2015030351 | ISBN 9781621902508 (pbk.)
Subjects: LCSH: German shepherd dog—Tennessee—Anecdotes. | LeConte,
Mount (Tenn.)—History. | Camps—Tennessee—LeConte, Mount—History. |
Adams, Paul J. (Paul Jay)
Classification: LCC SF429.G37 A38 2016 | DDC 636.737—dc23
LC record available at http://lccn.loc.gov/2015030351

CONTENTS

Acknowledgments ix

Introduction xi
Anne Bridges and Ken Wise

CHAPTER ONE The Purchase of Smoky Jack 1
CHAPTER TWO Becoming Acquainted 11
CHAPTER THREE Our First Hike Together 23
CHAPTER FOUR Timber Wolf 33
CHAPTER FIVE Teaching Smoky Jack to Pack Supplies 41
CHAPTER SIX Chicken Attached to Collar 59
CHAPTER SEVEN Attacks on People 63
CHAPTER EIGHT Broken Leg 71
CHAPTER NINE High Trail Robbery 77
CHAPTER TEN Huggins Hell 89
CHAPTER ELEVEN Accident at Last Water 101
CHAPTER TWELVE A Nose for Tracking 109
CHAPTER THIRTEEN Work for Ramsey and Huff 115
CHAPTER FOURTEEN Down Mount Le Conte 131
CHAPTER FIFTEEN Smoky Jack to the Rescue 137
CHAPTER SIXTEEN End of an Era 153

Epilogue 163
Selected Bibliography 179

ILLUSTRATIONS

Smoky Jack with Saddle Pockets, Winter of 1932   xiv

Mount Le Conte with Gatlinburg in the Foreground   xvii

David Chapman   2

Andy Huff and Paul Adams   14

Will Ramsey   15

Charlie Ogle's Store in Gatlinburg   17

Frank Wilson, Smoky Jack and Paul Adams
on Mount Le Conte, 1925   31

Mountain View Hotel, Gatlinburg, 1926   43

First Log Cabin Built on Mount Le Conte, Winter of 1925–26   55

Camp on Mount Le Conte, 1925   78

Charlie Ogle's Store in Gatlinburg   85

Cliff Top, Mount Le Conte, August 22, 1937   91

Members of the Rotary Club on Mount Le Conte   100

Smoky Jack and Adams, Winter of 1925   102

Frozen Rainbow Falls, December 1925   104

Jack Huff in Front of Gatlinburg Post Office   119

Smoky Jack in Front of his Kennel atop Mount Le Conte,
Winter of 1925   123

Outdoor Kitchen on Mount Le Conte   128

Grassy Patch Cabin   132

Hikers at Jack Huff's Le Conte Lodge   142

Cumberland Jack II of Edelweis (a.k.a. Smoky Jack)
Grave Stone   178

ACKNOWLEDGMENTS

Anne Bridges and Ken Wise, the editors of *Smoky Jack,* would like to thank Jim Casada and David Brill for their careful reading of the original manuscript and insightful comments and suggestions. We hope the final product lives up to their expectations. Elizabeth Wilson and Noah Lasley provided invaluable assistance with the review and editing of the original manuscript. A special note of appreciation goes to Ilene Jones Cornwell, who helped Paul Adams with the manuscript and had the foresight to save both the original manuscript and the invaluable photographs that document Paul Adams's tenure on the top of Mount Le Conte. She later donated the collection to the University of Tennessee Libraries. Many of the photographs are included in *Smoky Jack*. The remainder may be viewed on the website of the University of Tennessee Libraries.

Above all, we want to thank Paul Jay Adams, who took the time late in life to record the memories of his time on Mount Le Conte. He recognized the value of his contribution to this most iconic Smokies landmark at a critical point in the development of the proposed Great Smoky Mountains National Park and ensured that his experiences would be preserved. And finally an affectionate rub on the head and a handful of dog biscuits to Smoky Jack, a dog like no other.

INTRODUCTION

On July 11, 1925, Colonel David C. Chapman, vice-chairman of the Great Smoky Mountains Conservation Association, announced that the Association had appointed a custodian to monitor visitors to the summit of Mount Le Conte. The Association aimed to preserve the mountain, anticipating its eventual inclusion in a proposed national park. To that end, the Association crafted an agreement with the Champion Fibre Company, which had previously purchased Mount Le Conte with the intention of logging the mountain. The new custodian, Paul Adams, a twenty-six-year-old outdoorsman with a keen interest in biology, was to be steward of the Association's agreement with Champion. His charge from the Association was to "protect plant and animal life," to "look particularly after sanitary conditions," and to "make visitors more comfortable."[1]

Born 1901 in Paxton, Illinois, to Nittie Elizabeth (Vanderhoff) and Rev. Clair Stack Adams, Paul was encouraged from an early age by his father to take regular Sunday afternoon walks and keep journals and notes of all that he saw. A summer's visit to the Ozarks on a family vacation awakened young Paul's awareness to the uniqueness of mountain ecology, and a serious pastime of collecting moths and butterflies extended his appreciation of the natural world.[2] By 1914, the Adams family had moved to Burnsville, North Carolina, where Paul developed his passion for exploring mountains, learning to fish the rushing streams, and identifying the birds, flora, and wildlife that lived in the highlands.[3] In 1918,

---

1. David Chapman, "To Whom It May Concern," 11 July 1925, Paul Jay Adams (1901–1985) Papers, 1912–1977, Addition I, box 3, folder 3, Tennessee State Library and Archives.

2. Adams's collection was given to the University of Tennessee but was later lost in a fire that destroyed Morrill Hall in 1934.

3. What follows on Adams's early life is taken from his journals. See Paul Jay Adams (1901–1985) Papers, 1918–1962, box 3, III-D-3, Ac. No. 967, Tennessee State Library and Archives and Paul J. Adams, *Mt. LeConte.* Knoxville: Holston Printing Company, 1966.

at age sixteen, his family moved again, this time to Knoxville, Tennessee, where Paul's attention turned to the Great Smoky Mountains once he had hiked to the summit of Mount Le Conte for the first time.

Adams entered the University of Tennessee as a special student[4] in 1923, but his studies were interrupted during his freshman year by a series of surgeries necessitated by a childhood history of illnesses. As was the case with many young people of that generation, doctors recommended that Adams suspend his schooling and spend the time outdoors in fresh air. The doctors' orders were sufficient excuse for Adams to spend his waking hours exploring the Smokies. Starting on the southwestern end, he traveled along the spine of the main Smoky divide, carefully exploring every ridge, trail, bald, and peak until reaching Davenport Gap at the northeastern end. Many ridges on the eastern end of the divide were not yet marked with trails and Adams had to explore by trial and error.

During his early years in Knoxville, Adams worked occasionally for Brockway Crouch in his Knoxville Florist Shop. Adams met Crouch through the Knoxville chapter of the Tennessee Ornithological Society and the two became close hiking companions. Adams was also occasionally accompanied on Smoky Mountain hiking adventures by F. B. Morgan, a reporter for the *Knoxville Sentinel*. It was through his acquaintance with Crouch that Adams became a charter member of the Smoky Mountains Hiking Club and through Morgan that he was introduced to Colonel David Chapman. Recalling his initial meeting with Chapman, Adams later wrote "my first impression of him was that he was a man of great integrity and fortitude, one who would achieve whatever he set his heart to do."[5]

Prior to Adams's appointment, Mount Le Conte was largely an unknown fastness rarely visited by anyone other than the occasional Smoky

---

4. Adams attended Tusculum Academy (now College) near Greeneville, Tennessee, from 1917–1918 and Knoxville's Young High School from 1919–1922. Ilene Jones Cornwell Papers, MS 2054, box 1, folder 11, University of Tennessee Libraries.

5. *Mt. LeConte.* p. 12.

Mountain hunter or outside adventurer. By 1924, with the formation of the Smoky Mountains Hiking Club and fortuitous visits by botanists from distinguished academic institutions, outside awareness of Mount Le Conte as a place of surpassing natural beauty harboring abundant plant species began to gain impetus. In the same year, the Great Smoky Mountains Conservation Association was organized with the mission of advocating for the establishment of a national park in the Great Smoky Mountains while promoting Mount Le Conte as the crown jewel.[6] The more fundamental objective of the Association was the promotion of tourism and, with it, the roads and service amenities that would further attract prospective visitors to the East Tennessee area.

Paul Adams's association with Mount Le Conte began in 1918 when he climbed the mountain by way of Mill Creek[7] and found on the summit an undisturbed forest enclosing a single rotting hunter's lean-to and a spring affording a reliable source of water. When, seven years later, Adams returned as custodian of the mountain, the frequency of human intrusion engendered by ever-increasing awareness and promotion now necessitated enforcement of conservation practices to protect Mount Le Conte from wanton destruction.

In the greater scheme of events, Adams's appointment marked the convergence of seemingly unconnected circumstances and developments that would eventually unfold in the formation of a national park in the Great Smoky Mountains, bringing with it an influx of tourists that would soon make the Smokies the most visited park in the country

---

6. Originally organized in October 1923 as the Smoky Mountain Forest Reserve Association, the name was changed to Smoky Mountain Conservation Association in January 1924 to reflect its mission for "the preservation of the remaining primeval forests in eastern America and a national park in the Great Smoky Mountains." On 5 June 1925, the Association was incorporated as the Great Smoky Mountains Conservation Association with a charter to raise funds for the purchase of land for a proposed park. See Daniel S. Pierce, *The Great Smokies: From Natural Habitat to National Park* (Knoxville: The University of Tennessee Press, 2000, p. 62–65).

7. Because of the number of streams in the Smokies named Mill Creek, the Tennessee Nomenclature Committee changed the name of this stream to Le Conte Creek with the advent of Great Smoky Mountains National Park.

SMOKY JACK WITH SADDLE POCKETS, WINTER OF 1932, CHILHOWEE MOUNTAIN. PAUL J. ADAMS PHOTOGRAPH COLLECTION. UNIVERSITY OF TENNESSEE, KNOXVILLE LIBRARIES.

and create demand for camping accommodations on the summit of Le Conte. In the more mundane, his appointment would mark the nascence of the famous LeConte Lodge that currently resides on the summit of the mountain, as well as the start of a long friendship with Smoky Jack, a large German shepherd that would be Adams's sole constant companion during his tenure as custodian of the mountain.

Adams purchased Smoky Jack soon after learning of his appointment as custodian. Named Cumberland Jack II of Edelweis at birth, the dog had been trained from a puppy as a police dog adept at following commands. Upon purchase, Adams changed the dog's name to Smoky Jack to reflect the anticipated association of the dog's life with the mountain. Nine months later when Adams was relieved of his charge on Le Conte, he changed the dog's name back to Cumberland Jack, tacitly registering his disappointment with the turn of events.

Adams never mentions the circumstances of his decision to return the dog's name to Cumberland Jack. Years later, when drafting the manuscript for this book as well as *Mt. LeConte,* a self-published account of his adventures as custodian on the mountain, Adams restricted the dog's name to Cumberland Jack, never alluding to Smoky Jack even though Adams is consistent in referring to the dog as Smoky Jack in a daily journal he kept during his time on Le Conte. The name Smoky Jack appears in captions of early photographs of the dog and in newspaper reports concurrent with Adams's tenure on Le Conte. With respect to the Smoky Mountain themes prevalent in the manuscript and in acknowledgement of the first name Adams chose for his faithful companion, the editors have opted to change the narrative to reflect the name Smoky Jack.

Smoky Jack is chiefly the story of a remarkable dog whose physical prowess and uncommon intelligence made him a fitting companion for the young Paul Adams living alone in the remote mountain wilderness. Emerging in unexpected places and wending in and out of the storyline are a wealth of fragmented particulars that suffice as primary source material on the history of both the older routes to the summit of Le Conte and the evolution of newer trails, the place of Le Conte in the boots-on-the-ground machinations behind the movement to establish the national park, its place in the earliest lore of the Smoky Mountains Hiking Club, and the contingencies that conspired to shape the future LeConte Lodge.

Smoky Jack and Paul Adams are both players in an anachronistic mountaineer micro-economy. Goods and services are bartered and sold; local mountaineers are retained *ad hoc* for hire; transport is largely upon "their own wethers"; and exchange is based on honesty with accounts kept on running ledgers. In many ways Adams's book chronicles events occupying the edge, the crease between the influx of outside forces introducing the prospect of change and progress against the rock-solid stability of the mountaineers adhering to their traditional backwoods way of life.

Adams likely never fully grasped the reason for his dismissal from Le Conte. "I shall not write the causes of losing my job for I do not know them, at least all of them, but I do not think I have been given a square deal."[8] There appears to be no evidence of conflict with Chapman or other members of the Association nor of any neglect of duties. However, in responding to a letter of inquiry shortly after Adams's termination, Chapman offers assurance that "we are trying to make things a little more comfortable on top of Mount Le Conte, a larger and a better cabin is just being completed. With this I believe we can at least keep people dry in case of rain."[9] While Adams's dismissal may not or may not be associated with issues of visitor accommodation, Chapman nevertheless replaced Adams with Jack Huff whose father, Andy Huff, was owner and operator of the Mountain View Hotel in Gatlinburg.

During his nine-month tenure as custodian of Le Conte, Adams made improvements that later become permanent fixtures on the summit of Mount Le Conte. The camp he established would quickly evolve into the compound known as LeConte Lodge. In the interest of increasing his guests' enjoyment of the mountain, Adams cut a path that is now the most popular access to Cliff Top, a superb vantage point from which to view Smoky Mountain sunsets.

Even with his dismissal, Adams did not relinquish his association with Mount Le Conte. He remained at his post until Andy Huff and Will Ramsey arrived to take over the management,[10] then reinvented himself as an informed guide escorting overnight visiting parties to the camp. Adams later solicited permission from Champion Fibre Company to construct another access to the summit by way of Grassy Gap, a course that survives in part as the Trillium Gap Trail.

Late in life and relying on memory assisted by notes from his daily journals, Paul Adams constructed an engaging, though somewhat disjointed, account of his adventures with Smoky Jack on the summit of

8. Journal entry for 11 May 1926, Paul Jay Adams (1901–1985) Papers, 1918–1962, box 3, III-D-3, Ac. No. 967, Tennessee State Library and Archives.

9. David Chapman to Vic Davis, 22 May 1926, Great Smoky Mountains Conservation Papers, box 14, folder 18, Great Smoky Mountains National Park Archives.

10. Journal entry for 10 April 1926, Paul Jay Adams (1901–1985) Papers, 1918–1962, box 3, III-D-3, Ac. No. 967, Tennessee State Library and Archives.

MOUNT LE CONTE IN THE DISTANCE WITH GATLINBURG IN THE FOREGROUND. THOMPSON BROTHERS DIGITAL PHOTOGRAPH COLLECTION, UNIVERSITY OF TENNESSEE, KNOXVILLE LIBRARIES.

Mount Le Conte. The manuscript was submitted to three publishing houses, but all politely declined. One editor responded with a comment that "there are definitely organizational problems in the manuscript that need to be overcome . . . The story lacks continuity: one reads a puzzling bit of information on one page, the explanation for which appears on the next page—that sort of thing."[11] Adams was not a practiced writer—his prose a bit stiff and stilted—nevertheless his style and tone are consistent

---

11. Carol Orr to Ilene Cornwell, 5 November 1984, Ilene Jones Cornwell Papers, MS 2054, box 1, folder 10, University of Tennessee Libraries.

throughout. One does not read the clumsily crafted journals of Lewis and Clark or Francis Parkman's *The Oregon Trail* because of the authors' command of language or scintillating prose. These books are read because they capture an important era in our history. *Smoky Jack* resonates in much the same way, presenting the exploits of a most remarkable dog and his master, who together trod familiar ground in an age long past.[12]

---

12. The editors did make some substantive changes. In addition to changing the name of the dog to Smoky Jack, we standardized the spellings of all of place names. To better illuminate the distinction between conversational text and text that is not conversational, we deleted all of the contractions in the non-conversational text. In addition, while we did not change Adams's distinctive voice, with the assistance of a copyeditor we added or deleted commas that sometimes bedeviled Adams's prose style and very occasionally changed words to conform to more standard English usage.

Smoky Jack

CHAPTER ONE

The Purchase of Smoky Jack

W hen I was assured by Colonel David C. Chapman[1] in 1924 that I would be appointed by the Great Smoky Mountains Conservation Association[2] to start a camp on top of Mount Le Conte, I started

---

1. David Carpenter Chapman (1876–1944), president of Chapman Drug Company and avid supporter of the proposed Great Smoky Mountains National Park, was vice-chairman and later chairman of the Great Smoky Mountains Conservation Association. In 1927, he was appointed chairman of the Tennessee Great Smoky Mountains Park Commission, an organization established primarily for the purpose of raising money to purchase land in Tennessee for the proposed park. Known as Colonel Chapman, he was assigned to the Tennessee National Guard in 1918 and charged with the formation of the Fourth Tennessee Infantry Regiment in East Tennessee.
2. Originally organized in 1923 under the name Smoky Mountain Forest Reserve Association, the Great Smoky Mountains Conservation Association was reconstituted the next year when "Forest Reserve" was dropped from the name and "Conservation" added. The change in name was made to reflect the organization's mission to promote the establishment of a national park in the Great Smoky Mountains. The Association's membership included some of Knoxville's more influential and civic-minded citizens.

looking around for a grown, intelligent dog which might be a companion to me there in my vigil.

At that time I did not own such an animal, and a dog gives a person of the outdoors a great deal of real companionship. It was mainly because my mother insisted that I have a dog with me in this project, a sometimes lonely life on top of a mountain, that I considered getting one. She told me that the Association should appoint two persons for such a job. I told her that this had already been discussed among the group's members and that it had settled down to one man or nobody at all. I told her that I wanted this position and wanted it badly enough to tell them that I would accept it by myself.

Mother had worried about me a few years before when I was caretaker for the Boy Scout Camp on Copper Ridge, and she had insisted then that I keep our dog, Guess, with me while I lived there for nearly a year.

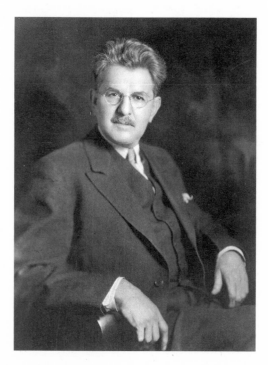

DAVID CHAPMAN. DAVID CHAPMAN COLLECTION, GREAT SMOKY MOUNTAINS NATIONAL PARK ARCHIVES.

Of course, mothers worry about their offspring. It is natural that they do so and mine was no exception. This worrying is particularly pronounced if their children are unattached—and getting married was far from my mind when the appointment was made. Our family was dogless at that time, Guess having died in 1923, and I had not acquired another. I told Mother that I would look around and try to find a grown dog to live with me. I talked this over with Colonel Chapman and he, too, thought it was a pretty good idea. "But for goodness sake," he said, "buy one that has a little sense and won't be an encumbrance, but instead, be a comfort and a companion."

A week or so before the appointment came through for me as custodian on Mount Le Conte, I called Russell Smith, a dog breeder in Knoxville, and asked him if he knew of a grown dog with intelligence I might purchase. He immediately said, "Cumberland Jack II would make your best companion, Paul."

"But I cannot afford that dog; he is too high priced. Is there another dog of like size that you know of for sale?" He thought a few moments and asked me to come to his home the next morning. We could go look at several dogs he knew of whose masters had tired of them. Perhaps I could find what I wanted from among them. Russell, a dog breeder and fancier, also boarded dogs for their masters when they were on vacation.

I drove out to Russell Smith's the next morning and, when I walked up to his dog pens where he was feeding the animals, Cumberland Jack II barked loud and long as I approached. I walked into Jack's running yard and played with him a few minutes while Russell went about other duties. When he called to me that it was time for us to be on our way, Jack followed me to the gate and wanted to tag along after us. I had to give him only one command to stay before going out of the yard. The dog looked longingly at us as we entered my car and drove away.

We looked at many dogs that day. Some dogs were vicious. Some were trained to be show dogs only. One shepherd caught my eye, but I was not sure he was the companion I needed.

As we drove back toward Smith's home, he told me that he would talk to the owner of Cumberland Jack of Edelweis to see if the asking price could be lowered. He thought that Jack would be my best buy. I told him to get that price cut in half and, if I could buy the dog on time, I'd take him. Otherwise, let's forget about him and buy the shepherd.

I had known Cumberland Jack for about a year. He was introduced to me when my friend and I were driving out Kingston Pike one day and stopped at a doctor's home to examine four dogs which had recently been returned from a veterinarian. The doctor wanted Russell to keep his eye on the dogs for a few weeks to see if they were getting along all right. As we entered the running yard that morning, I was warned about one of the dogs being a little vicious. The dog was pointed out to me, so I kept my distance. Another beautiful, nearly jet-black, short-haired German police dog was in the yard, too. I admired him very much and asked my friend if he belonged to the doctor. He told me to pet this dog if I wanted to. So stepping aside a little ways, I hunkered down and gave him one command, "come." The dog came to me and smelled me both front and rear. I then laid a hand upon him and petted him a little. Rising, I asked the dog to "heel." He immediately got behind me and followed me to the end of the running yard. There we stopped, and again I petted him while Russell examined all the other dogs. When it was time to leave, I told the black dog, "let's go," and he ran ahead of me to the high gate, where I told him goodbye. On our way on out Kingston Pike, Russell told me the history of this dog and he also said, "Don't get too familiar with him because you can never afford to own him."

Cumberland Jack had been bred of show-type parents near Cumberland Gap, Tennessee. While still a puppy he had come to live with Russell Smith, who put him up for sale when he was about a year old. This dog showed considerable intelligence and learned lessons well. Smith had sold him to a detective on the Knoxville police force who, after keeping the dog for a while, decided to send him to a police dog school in New Jersey to be trained for police work. He was there for about nine months. While Jack was being shipped back to Knoxville by express over the Southern Railway, his master was killed in a running gun battle with fugitives.

The dog was met at the station by Smith and taken to his kennels. The wife of the detective asked that the dog be put up for sale for a price of $500.00. He had been used in police work in Knoxville with Russell

Smith as his handler. He tracked down fugitives and murderers and was well liked by those officers who worked with him. There were no buyers for the dog. At that price, nobody seemed to want him. So he had two homes during the interim, at Russell's and at the doctor's. The detective's widow never saw the dog after her husband's death. She was afraid that she would become as attached to him as her husband had been and that she would want to keep him for her own. As time went on, there was no buyer for him, just police work, for which she received a fee once or twice a month as he performed the duties expected of him.

Cumberland Jack was a lovable dog, but he could be all business, too. When he was working, he listened only to his handler and explicitly obeyed the commands given him. I had seen the dog several times and in each one of these instances, regardless of how I was dressed, he smelled me thoroughly. I am sure that he did not smell any other dog on my clothes and I wondered about this at times. Perhaps he smelled the mountains and a free, happy-go-lucky sort of scent and wished that I would take him away with me where he, too, could run in the woods.

I did not hear from Russell for a few days. We had an agreement that if he could persuade the owner of the dog to meet my terms, I would buy him in preference to any other dog that I had seen or that had been offered me. I had almost given up hope of ever owning him when one morning Mother called me to the phone, saying that Russell Smith wanted to talk to me. I hurried to the phone, anxious to hear what he had to say. There were still doubts in my mind, but they were soon relieved. Russell told me that he had called Jack's owner the evening we had been out dog hunting and talked to her a long time. He told her that he had known me for several years and I was always kind to my dogs. He told her that I never punished a dog by whipping it. He told her why I wanted a grown dog, something about the position I was soon going to assume, and what I could afford to pay. She asked for a few days to think it over and just that morning had called Russell to tell him that I could have Cumberland Jack. From what I heard later, she had made other inquiries about me. Evidently, all those to whom she had talked had spoken very highly of me and told her that the dog would have a good home and that I would be good to him.

The terms of sale would be $50.00 down and $25.00 a month after the first of September, until he was paid for. The registration papers would be delivered to me at the end of the contract.

Russell wanted to know when I would be out to pick up the dog. I told him that I would come that very morning—right then, in fact, for my appointment had already gone through as of the previous day, and I wanted to take one load of supplies that day to Cherokee Orchard[3] in my car. The sooner I got the dog, the better off both of us would be.

After our phone conversation, I turned to Mother and my sister, Jean, and told them that the lady had decided to sell Cumberland Jack to me for a price of $250.00 to be paid on time, and that I would hurry out there before picking up supplies to take to Cherokee Orchard. Mother thought I was buying something that would give me trouble and she by no means liked the price. She said, "Paul, your father has bought good saddle and carriage horses a great deal cheaper than that. I cannot for the life of me see you paying so much for a dog. I just can't go along with it, and I know that when your father finds out about it, he's not going to like it either."

Jean had seen the dog. I took her out to Smith's one Sunday afternoon to help the kennel owner exercise his dogs. She had noticed that this particular dog had been very attentive to me. She told mother, "Yes, it is a large dog, Mother, and a beautiful one at that, and I think that the two will get along just fine. In fact, I wouldn't mind owning him myself if I had use for him. He's already trained and he has shown affection for Paul. I don't think that there will be trouble between them. I'm all for the deal."

I do not know which one of us was happiest that morning when I arrived at Russell Smith's, Smoky Jack or me [Adams changed the dog's

---

3. Cherokee Orchard was established as a commercial enterprise occupying a 796-acre tract immediately south of Gatlinburg and at the base of Mount Le Conte. Until purchased for the Great Smoky Mountains National Park in 1931, this tract of mountain land supported an apple orchard and ornamental nursery. After the discontinuation of the business, the name Cherokee Orchard survived as a Smoky Mountain place name. The trail to Mount Le Conte via Rainbow Falls started in Cherokee Orchard.

name from Cumberland Jack to Smoky Jack]. He seemed glad to see me and I know that I was glad to see him. All the dogs there had been fed and Jack had been placed in a running yard—or as Russell called it, a working pen—away from the others. If the truth were known, I think Russell had spoken my name to the dog when he led him to the pen, and perhaps this had something to do with the dog's attitude toward me. He barked loud and clear as I approached and, when I entered, he was right there at the gate to welcome me. Russell thought it best if he got completely off the premises while I was trying to work with the dog, so he drove around the city for more than an hour before returning.

Old Binkie, a powerful German police dog, one of the first of this breed Russell owned, walked over to one corner of his running yard and stood there watching Smoky Jack. The two dogs were mortal enemies and were never allowed to run together since a fight would always ensue. In fact, it was old Binkie, master of all the other dogs, who started the fights but Jack was no slouch when it came to dog fighting. Binkie had tolerated Jack until Jack had returned from police school. Then it was a different story. No wonder Smith had had to raise his fences to eleven feet and often he had to chain this oldest of the dogs, particularly when the two were in adjoining pens. In a way, I think that Smith was glad that Smoky Jack had been sold. It would mean more liberty for Binkie, who followed him so much of the time and was frequently taken with him to downtown Knoxville. Binkie did not have the nose that Jack possessed, nor had he been trained for police work. When Smith placed a heavy collar on Jack and led him away to help in trailing, Binkie could not quite understand why he was left behind.

Binkie stood there and watched closely as Jack and I worked together. Perhaps he was thinking to himself that he was going to get rid of this rival once and for all. I had known Binkie for several years. He was a stud dog and had taken his share of first prizes in many shows all over the country. He was an individual. There were not many persons who dared lay their hands upon him. Thank goodness, I was counted among his friends. He liked to be petted but never rousted with, never played with—such as boxing his ears and arousing in him the playfulness of other dogs.

As I entered the high gate, Jack was already there to greet me, wiggling all about, shaking his tail. He had been taught never to jump up on a person but to keep his feet on the ground, or if he jumped for joy, to do this without touching the person he was welcoming. I stood there and talked to the dog, squatting down at times and running my hands over his head and back. I tried to explain to him that I had come to take him away, that I hoped he would obey my commands, and that our lives together would be a great deal different than his had been for the past several months.

I gave him the command to "stay" when I arose and walked to the far end of the yard, about a hundred feet from the gate. In this walk I never glanced around to see if he had obeyed me. When I neared the opposite fence, I turned around to see the dog still in the position I had left him. I called to him to "come." He came, running fast to stand in front of me. I ordered him to "sit." He sat down on his haunches, looking into my face, wondering what the next command would be. I ordered him to "heel" as I walked slowly to the other end of the yard. He stayed four or five feet behind me, never once trying to gain upon me or get in front of me. I gave him other one-worded commands and he obeyed them all. I talked to the dog a great deal in this talk-and-obey session, knowing that I had to have him under my complete control within a very short period of time. Had he been a completely strange animal to me, perhaps I would have gone to Russell Smith's and worked him more frequently, instead of concentrating everything into such a short period of time. I even squatted down and petted him on his head and shoulders and back. I wanted him to become more familiar with me.

After about an hour and a half, Russell returned. I thought by that time I had the dog under complete control. He did not bark at Russell as the other six or seven dogs did. He stood beside me near the gate, and, as Russell approached, the dog wagged his tail only when spoken to. I started to open the gate, and Russell said, "Paul, you'd better reach up and get that chain and snap to his collar." I got the chain in my hand but did not put it on the dog. I said, "Russell, I have him under complete control and he will be chained very little as long as I own him."

Jack and I walked out of the yard. I walked toward my Model T, telling the dog to "heel." After I entered the car and sat behind the steering wheel, I invited the dog up on the front seat to sit beside me. He responded and happily wagged his tail in my face. I ordered him to sit and he sat down, head and ears erect, never once glancing over his shoulder as we drove toward the highway. This made me happy.

I drove the car across the Gay Street Bridge and had nearly reached the corner of Hill Avenue when Jack saw two uniformed policemen chasing a man. One of the policemen was using his whistle and the other was calling for the man to halt. The man did not pay any attention to either. He kept on running.

Smoky Jack became alert. He leaped from the slow-moving car and ran after them. I double-parked, grabbed a dog chain, and ran after all of them. The fleeing man had turned the corner off Gay Street onto Hill Avenue and was halfway down the block before Smoky Jack ran around him, wheeled quickly, and barked and growled at the man.

Of course, the man stopped dead in his tracks. When I ran around the corner of Hill Avenue, I saw the man with his hands and arms up in front of his throat, standing quite still. The two police officers were standing just back of this fellow. One of them told me that he expected Russell Smith, instead of me, since they both assumed that Smith was caretaker of the dog.

Luckily I knew both policemen, and, as they handcuffed their prisoner, I reached down and snapped the chain to my dog's collar. The policeman I knew best asked me what I was doing with the dog. I told him that I had just purchased him and was taking him to the top of Mount Le Conte with me. He had read in the morning's newspaper that I had been appointed by the Conservation Association to the new position and wished me success in the venture. He assured me that I had acquired a very valuable dog, one that would be surely missed when lawbreakers had to be trailed. All four of us walked back toward Gay Street, turned the corner, and continued toward Main. One policeman put in a call for the paddy wagon from a phone on the corner. Smoky Jack and I climbed in my car and drove up Gay Street toward home.

I made Smoky Jack lie on the floor of the car. He did not like this but he stayed there, looking up at me each time we had to stop for a hand-operated traffic signal, as if to say, "What did I do wrong? I have been trained to help uniformed policemen and I thought that was doing my duty."

When we had driven as far as the north end of Gay Street, I reached down, unsnapped the chain, and invited the dog to sit beside me again. I drove on out North Broadway, past Central Avenue, and turned left onto Kenyon Avenue to park in front of our home.

I snapped the chain to the dog's collar again, leading him up on the front porch of the house. Mother and Jean had heard me park and had come out to the porch as he pulled hard on the chain. He was as excited as they were.

He first walked over to Jean and looked up into her eyes as if to say, "You must be my new master's sister." He also smelled her and sidled up to her. I told Jean to reach down and pet him lightly.

Mother, who stood a little aside, made the remark that she thought I had purchased the largest dog she had ever seen.

CHAPTER TWO

Becoming Acquainted

Smoky Jack was a powerful black dog. At shoulder height he was twenty-six inches tall. His shoulder breadth was nine inches, and when I purchased him he weighed ninety pounds. There was just one small white spot on the front of his chest, nearly between his front legs. He was short-haired, with a rather bushy tail, and short-eared for his breed. There was a touch of gray in his lower legs and a fleck of gray on his cheeks. His usual stance showed that he had been trained to stand as a show dog. He was registered in both the United and American Kennel Clubs and his pedigree was quite long. His forebears had come from Germany four generations back.

While Jack and I were at home, I took out the springy rear seat of my car. I needed every bit of space to pack supplies for Cherokee Orchard above Gatlinburg for the construction of the camp on top of Mount Le Conte. I fastened securely a carrier on the left running board. The dog watched my every move. Jean led him around the house and back again.

It was between ten and eleven o'clock when I told Mother not to wait supper for us. If we had not returned from Gatlinburg by suppertime, I would eat between Knoxville and Sevierville.

I was expected at the army salvage store on lower Central Avenue, and I backed the car into the covered carport where the store's truck was usually kept. I chained Smoky Jack to the steering wheel as a safeguard. I thought the chain essential on this, his first store visit.

Three of the store clerks helped me load supplies into the car. We placed heavy cooking and eating utensils on the floor and covered them with a large twenty-by-thirty-foot tent. Then we loaded blankets and lighter objects. In the running-board carrier we placed axes, mattocks, oil and gasoline cans, and a few coal oil lanterns. I asked one of the clerks to put a first-aid kit in the front seat. When he returned he told me the dog had growled at him. Already, the dog was showing his attributes.

It was about noon when I drove along Gay Street with Smoky Jack standing on the front seat beside me. There were many people on the sidewalks. A few of them called to me to ask questions, and I answered them:

"Yes, this is my dog now."

"Yes, this is the first of several loads of supplies to be taken to Cherokee Orchard to start the camp on top of Mount Le Conte."

"Yeah, come up and stay with us after next Monday night. But you'd better bring your own food."

Farther up Gay I saw General Carey Spence standing on the sidewalk near his shoe store. I turned the car to the curb. He saw us approaching and stepped out toward the curb. As he put his hand out to touch the car, the dog growled at him. I told the dog to "stay." His ears dropped, but the general did not try to touch the car again. He had never seen the dog but had heard of some of his work and told me he was sure I had made a fine choice. He asked if this was the first load of supplies. I told him that it was, that we would have four loads altogether, and that we would take one load a day to the Cherokee Orchard. He wished me "Godspeed" as I drove away.

Since the car was heavily loaded, we did not progress quickly. Old Sevierville Pike was a crooked road leading through small communities and Bays Mountain, through Shooks Gap and Old Seymour, and finally into Sevierville. I knew of an eating place not far out of Knoxville and stopped there for lunch. I left the dog chained in the car.

The owner and I knew each other and he greeted me as I walked into his establishment. Soon after I started eating, everyone in the restaurant heard a loud bark, followed by threatening growls. I ran out of the restaurant, followed closely by the owner. We found, as I had already expected, Smoky Jack standing on top of the loaded car, snarling and growling at a group of youths who had approached too closely. Both the proprietor and I walked to the car. I was telling the dog to quiet down. For the third time that day, the dog was showing me that he was working for my interests. The proprietor and I asked the young men to stop bothering the car and the dog. They came into the restaurant and I told them this was the first load of supplies to be taken to the top of Mount Le Conte. They admitted they had tried to touch the car in order to tease the large dog, but they also said he seemed to be every place at once as they approached from all sides. They found out very quickly they could not put their hands on the car. The proprietor told the young men this was a very dangerous dog and had but one hold on a man, the throat. He had seen the dog before and knew it had been trained in a school for police work.

When I finished my meal, I went out to the car. Jack was lying on top of the load, glancing every now and then in different directions. We were waved on our way by bystanders as we left. Jack rode beside me in the front seat.

I drove on to Sevierville and then to Gatlinburg, where I stopped at the Mountain View Hotel to talk to my friend Andy Huff[4] for a few moments and to make reservations for Sunday night. I found Will Ramsey[5] there. He offered to go to the Orchard with me and help unload the car.

---

4. Andrew Jackson "Andy" Huff (1878–1949), a sawmill operator and proprietor of the Mountain View Hotel, was a prominent resident of Gatlinburg.

5. Will Ramsey (1906–1987), a Gatlinburg resident who as a young man worked as a guide leading visitors into the Great Smoky Mountains. Ramsey often assisted Adams at the camp on Mount Le Conte.

Andy commented that he agreed with my mother, whose opinion was that I had purchased a dog I would not be able to control.

As Will and I reached the car and opened the front door, the dog gave a low growl. I placed my hand on him and told him that Will was traveling with us. I got him to move over a bit so Will could occupy a part of the front seat. Keeping his eyes on Will, he reluctantly moved over close to me. Before we arrived at the Orchard, Smoky Jack was allowing Will to pet his head and shoulders. Will had a soft voice and talked quietly to the dog. I wanted them to become friends, for Will would play an important part in our lives for a long time to come.

At the Orchard, I chained Jack to a post while Will and I unloaded the car. The dog watched our every move. After unloading the car, I turned the dog loose for a few minutes and allowed him to run. He looked in vain for a telephone or power pole and, not finding any, settled for the

ANDY HUFF AND PAUL ADAMS, JUNE 26, 1926. LAURA THORNBURGH, PHOTOGRAPHER. GREAT SMOKY MOUNTAINS NATIONAL PARK ARCHIVES.

trunk of an apple tree, scratched a little on the ground afterwards, then came toward us ready to be off again.

Some children had come from a farmhouse close by and stood at a distance watching. Several mongrel dogs were with the children, but they made no attempt to get close to my dog. Jack did not seem to pay too much attention to them and not once did he stretch his chain to reach them. They remained at a respectful distance. Perhaps this was the first large dog they had ever seen.

During the drive back to Gatlinburg, the dog stood in the rear seat compartment. Will ran his hand back to him a time or two and the dog accepted his pats. When Will got out of the car, Jack came up in the front seat and we drove home, arriving there in time for supper. That night, I put Jack in the basement, preparing for him and leaving a pan of fresh water.

The next morning, Mother called to me and said that I had better come downstairs and control the dog because he was lying on the front porch and forbidding her to go out and pick up the morning newspaper and milk. I hastily put on a bathrobe and went downstairs. Mother followed me out to pick up the milk and the newspaper while I talked to my new companion. Examining a basement window later, I found that Jack had broken a pane of glass while jumping through the window.

That day was nearly a repetition of the one before. We drove to the army salvage store, loaded my Model T, picked up Will in Gatlinburg, and went on to the Orchard. As we approached Charlie Ogle's store,[6] I told Will that I thought we should stop and let Jack and Charlie get acquainted. I snapped Jack's chain to his collar and led him onto the store porch. I had an idea that if the dog was not too old to learn new things, perhaps we could teach him to pack supplies. But that morning I did not say anything about that idea. I merely wanted Charlie and Smoky Jack to become acquainted and get to know each other. Charlie and the other men around the store thought I had bought a very large unmanageable dog, one that might give trouble. But Jack let both Charlie and Ephraim, his father who was postmaster, lay their hands on him and pet him. Charlie asked me, "Why did you buy such a large dog? He's bigger than any dog I've ever seen. He's mighty big and powerful."

Right then and there I filled in Charlie and his father on the purchase of Smoky Jack, how he had been trained, about the work that he had already done, and that I wanted protection. Charlie agreed with me that the dog was large and strong enough to give me any protection I might need and perhaps he could be trained for other uses. Smoky Jack took a liking to Charlie and his father.

As we were about to leave the store, Will said, "Why don't you turn the dog loose to run for a few minutes outside, Paul?" I did. It was a

---

6. Charlie Ogle's store, in the center of Gatlinburg, was situated in the fork of the intersection of the current Parkway and River Road "At the corner of the Elkmont highway and the winding old river road is Charley Ogle's store—the E. E. Ogle Company, to be exact—a rambling affair of many buildings, containing a huge stock of all kinds of merchandise." See Jeanette S. Greve, *The Story of Gatlinburg* (Strasburg: Shenandoah Publishing House, 1931, p. 116).

CHARLIE OGLE'S STORE IN GATLINBURG LOCATED AT THE FORK OF THE ELKMONT HIGHWAY (THE CURRENT PARKWAY) AND RIVER ROAD. *FROM PI BETA PHI TO ARROWMONT: BRINGING EDUCATION AND ECONOMIC DEVELOPMENT TO THE GREAT SMOKY MOUNTAINS, 1910–2004.* UNIVERSITY OF TENNESSEE, KNOXVILLE LIBRARIES.

mistake. We all stood on the raised front porch as the dog made his way down the steps and, dog-like, smelled around the ground a little. The next thing any of us knew, a pack of four mongrel dogs came charging around from the rear of the store and attacked Jack. There was no bristling, no challenge made. The four dogs immediately charged. Jack took care of all of them and chased them up the river road toward Steve Whaley's hotel.[7] It was one of the shortest dogfights any of us had ever witnessed. Jack was so quick in his attack that the action was faster than the eye could follow. When they all started running and were past the store's extra building and storage house, I gave a loud whistle. Jack stopped, looked at the fleeing dogs, and came back to me. Everyone

---

7. Greve identifies Steve Whaley's hotel as "Beyond the store [Charlie Ogle's store], and on the shaded road that follows the Little Pigeon River is the Riverside Hotel, Stephen Whaley's comfortable place, where one gets a cozy lodging, good food, and use of a swimming pool nearby and a superb view of Mt. Le Conte from the wide verandas." Greve, *The Story of Gatlinburg*, p. 116–17.

who saw the short fight decided that I owned the master of any dog in the community. Charlie and Will told me that these four dogs always attacked this way, all together, all at once. I wondered if this action would ever take place again. I had things to learn.

At the Orchard I did not chain the dog but let him run free while Will and I unloaded the car. He stayed pretty close to us but did show some interest in barnyard fowl close at hand. I called the dog back.

On the way back to town, Will told me that Circuit Court met the following week in Sevierville and that many young men of the community would be there to watch and hear the court cases. He said he would try to find three or four who would help me carry the supplies up Mount Le Conte.

That night I put Smoky Jack on the small back porch of our home and placed his pallet and water pan beside him. Next morning he was lying on the front porch again. He had jumped over a seven-foot lattice on two sides of the porch: nineteen feet to the ground from the top of the lattice. He allowed my mother to go out and pick up the paper and milk this second morning. As she opened the front door to let herself back in, the dog dashed past her and came directly to my room where I was dressing. Later, I examined the dog for broken bones, particularly broken ribs. I could not find any. He seemed to walk and run naturally, as if nothing had happened.

I tried to get Mother to feed him, but Jack was reluctant to eat for her. I knew that there might be times when he would be in Knoxville for several days, and I wanted him to get used to Mother's feeding and caring for him in my absences. Mother had always fed our other dogs after the family had eaten, using scraps and dog biscuits and supplementary foods, twice a day. This morning I had to approve the food placed before Jack.

It was Saturday. The load from the army salvage store would be light that day. We drove first to a wholesale grocery house and picked up considerable foodstuffs. The dog watched as the men loaded the car. Later, at the salvage store, we removed a part of this heavy material and left it to be picked up that afternoon after we returned from the Orchard. Our trip to Gatlinburg and the Orchard was uneventful, except that Smoky Jack saw a rabbit run across the road in front of us. He pricked up his ears and made an attempt to jump, but I was too quick for him. I grabbed his collar with one hand and slowed the car. The rabbit was soon out of sight and I released my hold on Jack's collar. I had guessed that sooner or later Jack would want to jump out of the car after a rabbit running across the road in front of us, but I did not expect it would happen so soon.

We stopped again at Charlie Ogle's store and were met by Will Ramsey. We talked to Charlie and his father. Smoky Jack fully accepted Charlie this time and allowed him to pet him on the head, shoulders, and back and to run his hands over him. This friendly action on the part of the dog made me have a little more confidence in him. Perhaps he was learning that I wanted him to get acquainted with certain people and that it would be me who selected his friends. At least I hoped that this was true.

During our ride to the Orchard, Jack did not like riding between us on the front seat. He jumped up on the top of the load we were carrying and stretched out there.

On our return trip to Knoxville that afternoon, I was driving along between Gatlinburg and Pigeon Forge at a fast pace when a rabbit ran across the road in front of us. Smoky Jack was too quick for me this time and left the car, striking the steep shoulder of the road and plunging down a steep embankment. He tried to right himself but to no avail. I quickly stopped the car, backed it up, and called to Jack as he came out of the West Fork of the Little Pigeon River. He had turned all sorts of somersaults going down the steep embankment and had been unable to stop. I don't know if he had forgotten about the rabbit, but he came back to the car limping a little. As I opened the door to let him in, he seemed a little disgusted with himself. He never tried a trick like that again. He would prick up his ears and perhaps bark at a rabbit or other animal which ran across the road in front of us, but he never left a moving car for a chase. He had learned his lesson, once and for all.

We returned to Knoxville and loaded the rest of the food we had left at the salvage store. That night I decided I would take the dog to my room and let him sleep there. Perhaps being close to me would have a soothing effect. All day long we had been together, never out of each other's sight for more than a minute, so maybe he was content to be near me. In the wee small hours of the next morning, I heard a screen rip open and awoke in time to see the dog go through the open window to judge the distance to the ground from the roof of the front porch. I called to him but too late. He had started his leap. Rising quickly and putting on a bathrobe, I rushed downstairs and turned on the front porch light. I called to Jack and he came to me. He followed me back upstairs, where I snapped a chain to his collar. I don't think there was any need for it because he did not go out again until after breakfast.

I was not in any hurry to leave Knoxville on Sunday. I gathered up personal blankets, a typewriter, a duffel bag with extra clothes, a few reference books, a Bible, collector's bags and bottles, a dissecting set (for I expected to prepare birds or at least study skins while on the mountain), flashlights, crosscut saw, buck saw, and various other items. I also collected three guns: 32–20 rifle, a revolver with cartridge belt, and a 410-gauge shotgun.

Smoky Jack watched my every move. He followed me up and down the stairs and into the basement. Perhaps he knew we had spent our last night in Knoxville for a while. Mother and Jean went to Sunday school and church and returned. I told Mother that I would eat dinner at home and leave for Gatlinburg in the middle of the afternoon. Rain threatened, but none fell. Each time I walked out to the car to pack something, Jack followed. He would not let me get out of his sight. A little while before noon, knowing that he would not receive much exercise for some time, I took an old tennis ball and headed for a nearby pasture, tossing the ball and catching it as I walked along. The dog made several spiraling leaps into the air to grab it before I did, and after we entered the field I threw it a little distance, telling him to go "fetch." He did, bringing it back to me each time and laying it at my feet as if to say, "Throw it again, I'll go get it." He was an ordinary dog in this respect and we spent fifteen or twenty minutes in this exercise.

Jack and I left for Gatlinburg in the middle of the afternoon. I made one stop on the way, at the home of John L. Marshall between Sevierville and Pigeon Forge. I had become acquainted with John through

Colonel Chapman. He was a national park advocate and a Tennessee state representative from 1921–1926. I had promised to stop and see him if the Conservation Association decided to place me on top of Mount Le Conte. He, too, thought that I had purchased a very large dog, but he said that the dog would be a true companion, that he was young enough to be taught more, and that he thought I could do it. Jack and I did not visit long. As we left, John walked out to the end of the swinging bridge in front of his home, hollering to me after the dog and I had walked across it: "Paul, that dog knows how to 'break step' crossing a bridge. He's smart."

We arrived in Gatlinburg between four and five o'clock. Andy Huff told me to drive the car into his carriage barn at the rear of the hotel since rain still threatened. I chained the dog to a post in the hotel's backyard, gave him a pan of water, and went to a room at the rear of the hotel to freshen up a bit before supper. Coming back downstairs, I went first to see about Smoky Jack. He seemed perfectly content.

I walked around the hotel to the front porch, where I talked to acquaintances and hikers who were going to eat supper at the hotel before returning to Knoxville. Two of them told me they had found a new trail blazed near the top of Mount Le Conte and had followed it, knowing that I had had a hand in making it. They had found the Basin Spring[8] and looked over the territory where the camp was to be set up the next day. They told me that the next weekend they would be up to spend the night.

After supper, I went to the kitchen and picked up some scraps to feed Smoky Jack and added a few dog biscuits for him. Afterward, I took him for a short walk and led him back to the barn. I tried to explain to the dog that he was to spend the night here. I could not see any possible chance of his breaking out of the building. Both front and rear doors were barred from the outside. I also moved his pan of fresh water into

---

8. Basin Spring, the largest spring on Mount Le Conte, marks the headwater of Roaring Fork. Adams's camp on Mount Le Conte was provisionally known as the Basin Spring camp.

the building. During the night, rain fell in short showers. When I went downstairs at five o'clock the next morning, Jack was curled up in the front seat of the car. He leaped out as he heard my voice and came to me, stretched a little, and allowed me to snap the chain to his collar. Jack was ready for a new day.

CHAPTER THREE

Our First Hike Together

Animal psychologists tell us that dogs acquire the characteristics of their masters. If the master is mean and vicious at heart, so will be the dog, attacking both friend and foe alike. If the master treats the pet as a baby, the animal is inclined to become one and will like to be pampered. If the master is one of those easy-going fellows who seldom show their tempers to those around him, the dog will pick up this attitude.

I have never tried to analyze my own character. I have left this to friends and acquaintances. I was born and reared in a Christian home and was taught the precepts of the Protestant religion. I also was taught to be tolerant of any other person's religious beliefs and politics. There are too many other interests which attract friends to each other to allow religion and politics to separate us. Such avocations as hiking, camping, walks through wilderness areas, identification of various species of birds, animals, insects, reptiles, and plants, and the study of rocks and inanimate things, as well as gaining knowledge from one another, are always pleasant transmissions of intellect. I am not, and never have been, a "know-it-all." I have always considered that, when a person reaches such a stage, he is too good for this world and should be ready to pass on to the next.

At Cherokee Orchard on the morning of July 13, 1925, Smoky Jack stood around as Will Ramsey and I prepared packs to be carried to the top of Mount Le Conte by the three boys he had hired to help. I kept Jack chained while this was going on. He would be turned loose when we started up the trail. He turned his head from one aide to the other, cocking it a little, as we worked. Will and I wanted to teach these young men to pack supplies in the way that would be most comfortable to carry on their backs up the rather steep trail to the campsite. The trail was then known as Mill Creek Trail [the current trail along the creek is Rainbow Falls Trail]. When the National Park was established several years later, there were several creeks by that name within the boundaries of the park. The name of the creek was changed to Le Conte Creek.

When I unsnapped Smoky Jack's chain from his collar and carried it from a ring on my packsack, he jumped for pure joy. He seemed to realize we were going to new places. I looked forward to many happy days on the mountain with him and I believed that it would be only on rare occasions that he would have to be tied. Part of the time on this, his first hike up the mountain, he led the way, running in front of us. Sometimes he would come back and follow me.

Jack was a happy dog. He really appreciated his full liberty, and, although I do not think he knew what he was getting into, he seemed to understand that we were going to walk this time instead of riding in an automobile. Sometimes the dog would get ahead of us fifty or sixty yards, stop, look back in our direction, then make a dash toward us with such speed that it seemed that he would strike one of us. But he would stop abruptly, look up at me, turn around, and go forward again. He covered at least twice the distance of the packers going up the trail that morning. He did not stray too far from the trail. When he did, he would put his nose to the ground, sniff a little, and take a few steps away, as if trailing someone who had previously stepped off the trail. Then he would return, look at me, and go on ahead up the trail. Once in a while, he would "air-scent" with his head lifted high and his nostrils twitching from side to side, or he would put his nose to the ground and smell where some animal or large bird had crossed the trail the previous night. I do not think that he smelled anything unfamiliar to him since his stops were short. But he smelled the woods which would be his home for many months to come.

The Rainbow Falls Trail we ascended that morning was four miles long from the Cherokee Orchard to the Cliff Top of Mount Le Conte. Someone had put a sign near the bottom of the trail at the barn in the Orchard: "4 miles to the top of Mount Le Conte, by way of Rainbow Falls. 2 miles to Rainbow Falls." The sign was well lettered and spaced, but someone who had evidently gone to the top of the mountain this way had, upon his return, printed in crayon another 4 in front of the original, making it read 44. Many hikers laughed about this. Some of us tried to erase this extra 4, but occasionally someone would place it back on that sign. It was a steep four miles. A year earlier, when the Smoky Mountains Hiking Club[9] was formed, every member taken into the club had to ascend and descend Mount Le Conte in one day as a requisite for joining the club. For the inexperienced hiker, the hike up and down the mountain in one day was nothing to be sneezed at. Of course, the more a person hiked up the mountain, the more familiar he would become with the trail. Hiking up with hundred-pound packs got to be easy after we learned which foot to use first at certain spots on the trail.

From the barn at the Orchard, the trail ran up the north side of the stream filled with speckled trout. Not once did this old trail cross the stream. There is now a newer one that does cross it. For the first half-mile up this original trail, one walked between the Orchard on the left and the creek on the right. Then you entered a different kind of forest where massive hemlocks, red maples, basswoods, hardwoods, and the now-extinct American chestnut trees grew in abundance. An occasional

---

9. The Smoky Mountains Hiking Club was formed in 1924 after some of the interested parties climbed Mount Le Conte together. Charter members included Paul Adams, Jim Thompson, and Albert "Dutch" Roth.

Fraser magnolia could be seen, as well as massive tulip poplars and large beeches. There were some red oaks but very few pines in this valley.

Just above the Orchard property, we entered virgin forest and would not leave it for the remainder of our hike. Trees had not been cut for lumber above the Orchard. This area is considered a rainforest and in such forests are exposed rocks, many of them gigantic boulders weighing hundreds of tons, covered with lichen and moss. Some hardwood trees towered a hundred and fifty feet above their bases, forming a canopy for lower-growing shrubs and perennial plants. It would be almost impossible to name all the trees, shrubs, perennials, ferns, and lichens found along this trail. Each time one traverses it, he finds something new to look at in vegetation. Each month of the year, something not heretofore seen would be sighted.

For the first mile and a quarter above the barn at the Orchard, horses could be ridden up the trail. The end of this part of the trail became narrow and descended to Le Conte Creek. From here on, we started climbing. It was another three-quarters of a mile to Rainbow Falls, up an easy grade between large trees and boulders. This part of the trail had been used for generations to travel to Rainbow Falls.

About halfway between the end of the horseback trail and Rainbow Falls, a large poplar tree over six feet in diameter had blown down and lay across the trail. Notches cut deep with an axe had been hewn into both sides of it. The two foresters who worked for the Champion Fibre Company,[10] then owner of a large portion of the mountain, thought this the best way to circumnavigate this portion of the trail, instead of changing its course to go around either the exposed roots or the top of the tree.

We rested often on our way up the mountain. I usually called the halts and they became more frequent the farther we hiked. We were climbing

---

10. Established in 1906 by Reuben B. Robertson, Champion Fibre Company was a wood pulp operation based in Canton, North Carolina. By 1925, the company owned Mount Le Conte, as well as many other timber areas in the Great Smoky Mountains. After much legal wrangling, Champion sold approximately ninety thousand acres, including Mount Le Conte, to help create the Great Smoky Mountains National Park in 1931.

steeper grades now. Long before we could see Rainbow Falls, we heard the rushing water. Le Conte Creek was running a little full. There had been rain on top of the mountain and rain now threatened. Fortunately, it did not fall on us. We found galax in bloom below the waterfall and discovered a few late-blooming blue cohosh. Doll's eyes had long since blossomed and were setting their white fruit. Blackburnian warblers were singing overhead in some of the large hemlock trees in which they nest. Near this more than eighty-foot waterfall, we encountered our first giant rosebay rhododendron in bloom. These are the tallest of irregular-growing evergreen shrubs, the large white-with-pink-tint blooms abundant. We rested at the falls, both below and above. Our trail ran on a rock ledge to the rear of the falls and then up through rhododendron thickets, where we not only needed our feet but our hands to help us gain higher ground. Jack helped himself by taking hold of branches and roots with his teeth. The trail around and just above the falls was soggy with water seepage from the high bluff. Above the elevation of the falls, we turned abruptly left and walking became easier. Soon we were back to Le Conte Creek and I wondered if Jack would jump the stream or wade it. He measured the distance with his eye, made one long jump, and he was across the creek before we stepped upon stones laid here by some earlier hiker to make the crossing easier for those who followed. A good hiker will not wade through water and get his feet wet unless necessary. As soon as we had crossed the stream, we took our packs off and rested. I took the boys off the trail a little way to let them look over the bluff near the waterfall. There they could see into the valley below and try to spot the top of Bullhead Mountain to our left, almost even with us in elevation.

Above Rainbow Falls are many crossings of the stream and its tributaries. The main stream becomes smaller as one ascends. For the next quarter of a mile, we had easy climbing. The trail rose steadily along the side of Le Conte Creek. Just above a crossing to the left-hand side of the stream, the trail led through a rock bar of large boulders. "Gray-backs" is the name used for such areas of tumbled rocks and these were tumbled in an area of perhaps twenty acres. Here the creek tumbled, too, and miniature waterfalls were abundant. Another crossing goes to the right-hand side of the stream and around a clay and shale bluff in a zigzag manner where Twin Falls can be seen plainly from both below and above.

A mile or so above Rainbow Falls, there is a change of vegetation. The hardwoods die out and evergreens are more common. Mountain laurel and rhododendron thin out. Yellow birches are common. Many species of viburnums, bush honeysuckle, small stunted serviceberries, mountain ash, fire cherries, and the ever-present mosses and ferns are abundant. We were above the range of some of the birds frequenting lower altitudes. We could hear the incessant call of the red-breasted nuthatch. Veeries cried out above us. Just before we came to the last creek crossing, where the switchback trail begins, there was a rather large, "stilted" yellow birch and a red spruce growing out of a crotch in the tree. This crotch was about twelve or fifteen feet above the ground. The spruce had sent a root down toward the ground and took sustenance from it as well as from the birch. The birch was an old tree and very gnarled. Just above this crotch is what we used to call the "Last Water," where the trail left the stream and led upward in almost a forty-five-degree angle. It had many switchbacks. This Last Water was, and still is, a dangerous spot. Just after crossing the stream, one has to traverse a wet clay bank. Water oozing out of the clay makes walking difficult in any season and there is nothing to hold onto to keep from slipping and falling. Footsteps have to be taken cautiously and the hiker has to be particularly careful going up and going down. I learned my lesson here one night the latter part of December 1925. Afterward, when this place was reached, I, like the dog, took a shortcut.

Smoky Jack leaped most of the creek crossings. He would wade through some of the wider ones. He would leap over, turn around and watch the rest of us cross the stream, and then go on up the trail. He never seemed to tire of trotting ahead of us and almost getting out of sight in this evergreen part of the trail. Then he would turn around and make a fast run back toward us, only to put his "brakes" on and skid to a stop a few feet in front of me. I never kept track of the times he did this. The boys told me that Jack would be worn out before we were. But, from all indications, he was greatly enjoying himself. Perhaps this was the first time he had been turned loose in the woods in his life. He was taking advantage of it and did not seem to tire. I often spoke to him, encouraging him to lead, trying to tell him that these woods would be our home for many months to come. I knew from his actions that he was enjoying himself.

About halfway up the switchback trail, between where we had left the stream for the last time and Cliff Top, the dog hesitated at a fork in the trail. He was standing there a little puzzled. The day before hikers had gone both ways at this spot. The dog put his nose to the ground and sniffed a few feet in both directions, only to turn around and come back to the fork. He had found the place where Marshall Ogle[11] and Will Ramsey and I had blazed a new trail into the original one. After much smelling, he looked down the trail at me. I gave him a hand signal to turn to the left. He started that way but sat down in the new trail and waited. He could not smell me here. It had been several weeks since this new trail had been blazed and my scent had been washed out of my footprints. Here at the forks we rested again, sitting in the cool evergreen forest. I told the boys that this would be our last rest, that the new blazes marked an easy grade. (Later we would clear the path and make a trail along the blazes.) The dog was a little hesitant in leading us. Instead he followed me closely to the campsite. Only once or twice did he venture ahead of us.

After half a mile of this evenly elevated climbing, I called a halt. We put our packs down and started taking out some of the buckets and containers in which we could carry water from the Basin Spring to where we would prepare our lunches. After emptying our packs, we walked out a little farther. I showed the boys the Basin Spring, gushing out from between rocks in a shallow valley less than a hundred yards from where we had taken off our packs. The boys looked around and commented on an old lean-to which stood nearby. I told them that I had helped repair this for a week's stay on the mountain in 1918. Then everyone coming to hunt also had made some repairs on it.

---

11. Marshall Ogle (1905–1969), a native of Gatlinburg, was employed by Adams during his tenure on Mount Le Conte.

During the afternoon, while two of the boys hiked down to the Orchard for more supplies, Lavater Whaley[12] and I erected the tent, made one balsam bed the full length of it, and stored our supplies. Smoky Jack did not get in our way as we worked. He did not stray too far from camp but continuously watched us. As Lavater ditched the tent so that rainwater would not run under it, I busied myself making an improvised table and cutting firewood. Just about dark Jack came to me. He sidled close and gave a low growl. The two boys were hurriedly walking toward us, empty-handed. As they neared, Jack recognized them. When he did, his attitude changed from one of protectiveness to one of friendliness. The boys said that since dark was approaching they had left their packs in the trail above the Last Water crossing and hurried on into camp. Lavater and I exchanged glances as he asked them why they did not bring their packs on into camp since they had flashlights with them. He also asked them why they had not hung their packs in trees where "varmints" could not get into them. The boys did not answer.

Smoky Jack did not sleep in the tent with us that night. He preferred to crawl under the table we had made. Rain fell during the night, but we remained dry. The next morning, all three boys walked down the mountain to bring up more supplies. Smoky Jack and I were busy about the camp before I started marking a trail toward the old campsite beneath Cliff Top and a branch of it which needed to be brushed out. It was not in very good shape at the time. I had been told to tear down the shack which stood there and decided that the four-foot seasoned puncheons could be used to good advantage in our new camp. Smoky Jack made explorations for himself that morning, returning to me every ten or fifteen minutes. I would speak to him, pet him a little, and then go about my business.

About noon, Jack ran rapidly toward me from the direction of our new camp, sidled up close to me, and growled as he faced the direction from which he had come. I looked and saw Lavater walking up our newly

---

12. Perry Lavater Whaley (1907–1987), a native of Gatlinburg, was Adams's assistant while on Mount Le Conte. Whaley later became a streetcar operator in Knoxville.

FRANK WILSON, SMOKY JACK AND ADAMS BELOW BULLETIN BOARD, CAMP ON MOUNT LE CONTE, 1925. FRANK WILSON (1910–1979) WAS FROM KNOXVILLE. HIS OLDER BROTHER MARSHALL WAS A CHARTER MEMBER OF THE SMOKY MOUNTAINS HIKING CLUB. PAUL J. ADAMS PHOTOGRAPH COLLECTION. UNIVERSITY OF TENNESSEE, KNOXVILLE LIBRARIES.

hacked-out trail. As Lavater walked up to us, Jack recognized my helper. The dog seldom barked. If he heard someone coming up the trail and I was outside, he would come to me, face the direction from which the person was coming, and give off low growls. He must have been trained to do this. About the only time he would bark at someone's approach would be when the door of the shack or cabin was shut, and he could not see me. Then his warning would be a rather loud, sharp bark. I responded whenever I heard it. He continued this method of letting me and my parents know of the presence of strangers. I have never known him to go out and continuously bark at someone as many dogs will do, challenging their approach. On rare occasions, he would approach a person whom he recognized, barking a little when doing so, but these barks were signs of gladness and happiness and were friendly in tone.

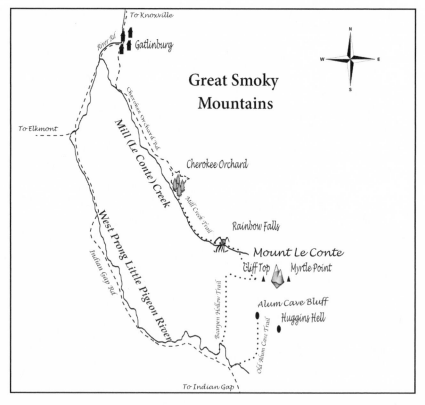

GATLINBURG AND MOUNT LE CONTE, 1925–26.

CHAPTER FOUR

Timber Wolf

Smoky Jack and I had lived on top of Mount Le Conte only a few days when he had his first encounter with a timber wolf. We were by ourselves at the time. The day was clear and warm. I needed a few long, slender balsam and spruce poles to cut into shorter lengths for table supports and lockers for supplies and food storage. I was in the woods toward Cliff Top, cutting away with saw and axe. Jack had accompanied me to the cutting area before romping off into the woods by himself. Suddenly, I heard Smoky Jack, running as fast as he could in my direction.

He was in such a hurry this time that he ran past me before he could stop. From the same direction in which he had come, I heard something else running very fast. I drew my revolver and cocked it, ready for action. A lone timber wolf came bursting out of the tangle of blooming hobblebush, ferns, and bush-honeysuckle, intent upon catching Jack. When he saw me facing him, the wolf skidded to an abrupt stop within fifteen feet of us. He saw the dog standing close to me. Jack ruffed up and growled loudly. I believe that the wolf was scared by the dog's actions. He wheeled sharply and disappeared into the woods. I returned my gun to its holster. At such close range, I could have killed that wolf. I surmised from Jack's running that he had been about a hundred yards in front of the wolf. I do not think that the wolf would ever have caught the dog. If the two had had a fight, Jack would have killed it, for the wolf appeared to have been underfed and certainly was much lighter in weight than Smoky Jack.

The first time I saw the wolf was in June 1924. I had hiked from Indian Gap toward Mount Kephart,[13] having spent the night at Icewater Spring. The next morning I retraced a part of my trail from the previous day and hiked out to what is known as the Boulevard, the ridge connecting Mount Kephart with Mount Le Conte. Hiking was slow, but I had been this way before and found many broken bushes along the way to show that others also had been there. A few limbs I had broken myself. This was a common habit for hikers exploring new territory, a forest tract where a well-defined trail did not exist. In this way, we were able to guide ourselves through trackless forests.

At Alum Gap, I shed my pack and sat down near it, my rifle across my knees, and looked at a beautiful view of tumbled high ridges to the north toward Porters Flat and the main high ridge of the Great Smokies. A nearby movement caught my eye and I looked to see the cause. There was a lone wolf running in an easterly direction about a hundred yards from me. Where was the rest of the pack? I had always seen wolves in packs, but this wolf was alone. I do not think that the wolf ever saw me or even sensed my presence. It never turned its head to look in my direction. I brought my rifle slowly to my shoulder and aimed at the animal. Then I thought to myself, "You can't eat it, so why kill it?" I lowered the gun and sat quietly while the wolf ran out of sight.

---

13. Mount Kephart was officially designated by the United States Geological Survey in 1931. In the 1920s, the peak was known provisionally by several names, including Mount Alexander.

A couple of months later, on the first Park Commission trip,[14] I asked men who had acted as guides and helpers if they had seen the wolf. Some of them said that they had seen this lone animal. One man told me he thought that he killed it one time but, when he arrived at the spot where he thought the wolf had dropped, there was no wolf nor could he see where it had gone. Those who had seen it, and shot at it, told me that it had been ostracized from a pack that still ran on the North Carolina and Tennessee sides of the Great Smokies, farther to the east and north. They were surprised to learn that I had seen the wolf in the vicinity of Mount Kephart and Mount Le Conte. It had never been known to go into the settlements by itself and kill domestic animals, as a wolf pack will sometimes do. The outcast wolf stayed in the virgin timber and lived alone. Perhaps this was one reason why rabbits were not common around the top of Mount Le Conte.

Smoky Jack and I were to have more experiences with this lone wolf. I do not think that Smoky Jack ran from any other animal. If he did, I never knew it. Usually when that wolf got after Jack, he came from the direction of Maintop[15] or Cliff Top, never from below the camp on the Le Conte Creek side. As time went on, and the camp yard was cleared of undergrowth for a fifty-yard radius, the wolf would never come into that area when chasing the dog. I could always tell when the wolf was after him by the way Smoky Jack approached me. Many visitors to the

---

14. Park Commission refers to the Southern Appalachian National Park Commission. The hiking party included Harlan P. Kelsey from Salem, Massachusetts (member of the Park Commission); Arno B. Cammerer, assistant director of the National Park Service; G. F. Pollock, president of the Northern Virginia National Park Association; David Chapman, Tennessee Great Smoky Mountains Park Commission; J. M. McLean, editor of *Southeastern Christian Advocate*, of Athens, Tennessee; Russell W. Hanlon, secretary of the Knoxville Automobile Club and Great Smoky Mountains Conservation Association; John Ottinger of *The Knoxville Journal*; F. B. Morgan of the *Knoxville News-Sentinel* and publicity manager for the Great Smoky Mountains Conservation Association; and Knoxvillians B. L. Johnson, J. C. Harris, Paul Schroeder, Ross Herd, Harvard Hunter, Charles N. Sharp Jr., and M. R. Sharpe.

15. Maintop is the provisional name by which Adams identifies the highest point on Mount Le Conte. Maintop is now officially known as High Top.

top of the mountain saw him and some asked why I did not shoot him. My reply was that he was an added attraction to the environs of the top of the mountain and Jack always won the fast race.

I know the wolf prowled around camp when there was no one there, for we often found his fresh footprints in mud and snow, but he never entered the tent or my shack. Perhaps the human scent around these places was too disturbing to him. His chasing Jack was always done in the daylight hours, never at night. In the depth of winter, I saw the wolf a couple of times in the early morning hours around the eating tables. When the snow was so deep that hikers could not climb the mountain, and I could not get off of it because of the snow, I saw the wolf twice. Being a bird-lover, I had cut two peek holes in the cabin walls to watch the ravens which occasionally visited the camp in winter. Through the peek holes, I saw the wolf near the tables. It was always on the move, rarely hesitating as a dog would in its search for food. Once it picked up a rather large meat scrap with the bone attached. Instead of stopping to eat it on the premises, the wolf carried it into the woods. I later found remnants of the chewed-on bone two hundred yards from camp. The large knuckle joint had been completely gnawed off the harder part of the bone. On bitterly cold mornings, the wolf would pass near the camp yard. I noticed that it never overturned a trash basket to examine the contents as a dog or bear might have done.

Later, Smoky Jack and I were hiking up the Le Conte Creek Trail[16] when I overtook L. Caesar Stair Sr. and his two young sons climbing the mountain. Mount Le Conte was one of the boys' favorite mountains to climb and their father believed in getting his children into the woods and teaching them about our great outdoors. I have always admired parents who take their children into the woods and fields and go camping with

---

16. At the time of Adams's tenure on Mount Le Conte, the trail to the summit of the mountain by way of Rainbow Falls followed Mill Creek. With the advent of the National Park, the name of the stream was changed to Le Conte Creek and the trail became known provisionally as the Le Conte Creek Trail. The trail was later officially designated as the Rainbow Falls Trail.

them. The boys, Richard and L. C. Jr., ran circles around us. I had done a little hunting on my way up the mountain and had killed a few gray squirrels below the waterfalls. Perhaps it was the sharp report of the rifle which attracted the Stairs' attention. When Jack and I caught up with them, they were sitting on rocks near Rainbow Falls. We exchanged greetings and hiked together up the trail. A short distance above the falls, the boys asked their father's permission to go ahead into camp. He consented but told them not to go any farther and not to go out to Cliff Top. They were soon out of sight. Caesar Stair and I hiked on up the mountain with Jack in the lead. In about an hour's time, the boys came back down the trail to meet us. The boys were both very excited when they approached us.

"How many dogs have you got, Mr. Adams?" one of them asked.

"Only Smoky Jack," I replied.

"But we saw another one," one said. "It was larger and had longer hair than Jack."

The boys told us that when they arrived in camp this animal was prowling around the eating tables and seemed very restless. They had whistled at it and tried to follow it into the woods, but it ran so fast they could not keep up with it. I told the boys they had seen a wolf. Their eyes opened wide. We walked on up the trail, the boys staying close to us.

One late-autumn morning, I wanted fresh meat. Smoky Jack and I walked north around Maintop and started down the long ridge leading to Trillium Gap and Brushy Mountain. There were many rhododendron thickets to skirt and the area was untracked. I had been over it many times and knew just which side of the ridge would be best to skirt those thickets and come back to the main ridge. I wanted to go down below the balsam and red spruce forest and work my way through the hardwoods toward Trillium Branch, a tributary of Cannon Creek, and up the mountain. I was sure that I could find gray squirrels and grouse in the area. Jack and I returned to the ridge, going around the last rhododendron thicket before turning eastward.

Smoky Jack sensed danger ahead. He trailed me by a few feet, instead of running ahead. I cautiously picked my way through the trees. We were now below the evergreens. Every few steps I stopped and looked in all directions. Jack was treading quietly, stopping when I stopped, just a few feet behind me. I did not speak to him, but it was not long before I found why he had taken a rear position. I saw the old timber wolf stalking a small covey of grouse just ahead. He was within fifty or sixty feet of the birds. The wind was blowing uphill and we were so quiet he did not sense our presence. I raised my rifle, took aim at the grouse closest to us but in front of the wolf, and shot. At the crack of the rifle, the wolf jumped straight into the air, hit the ground, and went running off into the direction of Rocky Spur.[17] Jack and I watched him disappear into the timber. We picked up the grouse and went on down the ridge. Smoky Jack wanted to go ahead of me now, but I told him to "heel." We went cautiously down, and before long I had another grouse tied to my belt. It was time for us to turn east and start hunting up the mountain. I let the dog go ahead of me and Jack treed several squirrels. Before we arrived back in camp, I added another grouse to my belt and had ten squirrels.

It was a beautiful sight to watch that wolf stalk grouse. I am sure he would have caught a meal for himself if we had not come along. Many times in my life, I have watched foxes stalk their prey. A few times on this same ridge, I have broken up such hunting, particularly if the fox was after young birds feeding with their mothers.

The last time I saw the outcast timber wolf was in 1929. I was leading members of the Smoky Mountains Hiking Club from the top of Mount Le Conte toward Balsam Point and the Bullhead. Smoky Jack was carrying his saddle pockets [see chapter five] with part of our provisions. He had been leading and was ahead of us, when suddenly he stopped and "air-scented." I walked up to him and saw wolf tracks leading toward Balsam Point. The tracks were plain in four inches of snow. The next day, I led the hikers to the top of Balsam Point. A fellow hiker, Smoky Jack, and I were some distance ahead of the slower hikers. We had brushed

---

17. Several years after Adams left Mount Le Conte, the trail above Rainbow Falls was rerouted away from the stream and up along Rocky Spur, a powerful ridge extending from the north flank of the mountain. The spine of Rocky Spur is marked by an open sand myrtle garden.

off a long log to sit on and enjoy the view. We were looking north from the top of a high bluff, when my companion whispered, "What sort of animal is that at the foot of the bluff, running by itself and heading back toward Rocky Spur?"

I whispered, "It's a wolf." It was slipping silently through the forest, exactly as it had been the first time I had seen it five years before.

CHAPTER FIVE

Teaching Smoky Jack to Pack Supplies

During the first two weeks after establishing the camp on top of Mount Le Conte, Smoky Jack and I made several hikes down and up the mountain. Jack had become accustomed to the trail and had started to make his own shortcuts. The two boys I hired for the summer's work had noticed this, too, and commented on it. We had made the Le Conte Creek Trail a little easier to climb by improving sections, widening the trail in some places, and placing large rocks on which to step in the airy areas, but we had not built any handrails to help hikers. We scouted areas near the large rock bar through which the trail passed, but we found that the original trail as laid out was still the best route. So we did nothing to change this section.

One evening about two weeks after the camp was established, Wiley Oakley[18] and Will Ramsey arrived with a group of visitors who had hired them as guides over the Le Conte Creek Trail to the mountain top. The return was scheduled for the next day, by way of Alum Cave Trail down to Dave Ogle's store,[19] where cars would meet them, and then back to the Mountain View Hotel where they were guests. There was a large pyramid-shaped campfire near the tent and Wiley was sitting there telling the visitors some of his tales. Will, Earnest Ogle,[20] and I were off to one side talking among ourselves about the future of the camp. It was costing us about four cents a pound for supplies brought into camp from the Orchard. I had an idea in the back of my mind that Smoky Jack might be taught to bring small items into camp from Charlie Ogle's store. I asked Will what he thought of the idea.

Will answered, "Smoky Jack is a young dog and he is learning things up here. He was taught things in police school and I think he can be taught new things. But how are you going to do it, Paul? Each time you and he go to town you drive down and back in your car."

"There is a shorter way, an old road that cuts off a good half-mile between the store and Orchard," he added. "You and he are going to have to stick to that original road. The dog knows his way perfectly well from the Orchard to the camp and, if he can learn the shortest possible route, it will be better for him to go and come that way. Perhaps we should walk this old road together. Jack has many shortcuts from the Orchard up. You and I have both noticed this. I believe he can be taught to pack small items into camp by himself. He is going to take the shortest distance between the two places."

I was happy Will had made the suggestion. Earnest also thought that Jack might be trained to pack. We agreed to meet at Ogle's store a few days later. Will was waiting for us when we arrived. Earnest left the store and drove my car, loaded with supplies, to the Orchard. Will, Jack, and I started up the shortcut. This way was nearly impassable for

---

18. Wiley Oakley (1885-1954), a native of Gatlinburg and self-styled "Roamin' Man of the Mountains," was a well-known Smoky Mountain guide and famed storyteller.

19. Dave Ogle's store stood in the Sugarlands along the old Indian Gap Road opposite the current trailhead for the Huskey Gap Trail.

20. Earnest Ogle (1906-1979) was a young resident of Gatlinburg who occasionally assisted Adams at the camp on Mount Le Conte.

MOUNTAIN VIEW HOTEL, GATLINBURG, 1926. ALBERT "DUTCH" ROTH, PHOTOGRAPHER. ALBERT "DUTCH" ROTH DIGITAL PHOTOGRAPH COLLECTION, UNIVERSITY OF TENNESSEE, KNOXVILLE LIBRARIES.

automobiles, except those having high rear systems. The old road had been washed out in many places. Since the new road to the Orchard had been constructed in 1923, the old one had become a road of the past. We had walked to a spot above the present location of the Methodist Camp Ground when we came to a clapboard house. The structure itself was set back from the road perhaps a hundred feet, with grass growing in the front yard surrounded by a four-foot stone fence.

Before we arrived in front of this house, we heard the barking of dogs. Will and I knew we would soon be challenged. The dogs came through an open gateway in the stone fence and charged toward us. Smoky Jack, who was leading us, stopped and was challenged immediately. It was not a long dogfight. Smoky Jack put the dogs in flight. He chased them as far as the fence opening, then stopped and turned around to return to us. We walked farther up the road.

About a mile above the house, Will told us we would have to pass another house where there also were dogs. When we neared the yard, out came four mongrel dogs, a little larger than the ones at the first house. They were hell-bent to find out who was coming up the road. They challenged Smoky Jack, who tried to avoid another fight by standing his ground and growling at them. The largest of the dogs took hold of Jack's flank and he was forced into another fight. He reached around, grabbed this dog by the nape of the neck, and shook him thoroughly. The companions of this large mongrel took up the fight at once, with Jack in the middle of the fray. As Jack got the better of the four dogs, they ran back to the safety of their home territory. They stood near the house and barked for quite a while.

As Will and I drew even with the yard gate, we saw one of our friends standing on the porch. He invited us in. He had heard his dogs and had seen a little of the fight, with Smoky Jack getting the best of it.

The man wanted to know why we were walking along the old road. We told him we were trying to teach my dog the existing shortcuts before training him to pack supplies to the top of the mountain. This man was also a guide, often hired by Colonel Chapman and other visitors to the mountains. He told us he would see to it his dogs never again attacked mine. He invited us in to sit "a spell," but Will and I thought it best to continue on up the trail. As we talked, his dogs stood back of him growling and snarling. Jack stood beside us outside the fence, ears alert, but he made no attempt to enter the yard or continue the fight. He was not interested. They had run from him. He was master of the day.

We walked on up the woodland road. Will said, "Paul, it might not be a bad idea for you and Smoky Jack to walk up this old road a time or two after you have saddle pockets for him."

My answer was, "Yeah, I'm going to do that. Perhaps Earnest or Lavater had better make a trip with him. Maybe you could make a trip or two with him." I also told Will if the dog could be taught to go between the top of the mountain and Ogle's store, "I want him taught." When we arrived at the Orchard, I packed one of my packsacks with supplies Earnest had hauled there. Then Jack and I hiked up the mountain. Will hiked on to his home across Scratch Britches Ridge, a shortcut that omitted going through town.

A few days after this, I returned to Knoxville where I gave Colonel Chapman some money and a progress report. I told him I was going to try to teach my dog to pack small articles up the mountain and thus reduce the cost of items delivered there from Gatlinburg and the Orchard. The colonel thought I might to able to do it. He talked of how army dogs in World War I had been taught similar duties. He cautioned that it would take time on the part of dog and master.

Smoky Jack and I drove from the colonel's office down to the army salvage store, where I had asked the proprietor to hold a heavy sheepskin coat for me. I needed supplies, too. As we walked around the store, I saw a cavalry officer's leather cases—one for maps, the other a briefcase—hung over the horn of a saddle. They were in an enclosed glass case, and I asked the proprietor to get them out for me to see. I noticed that the rawhide laces between the two bags were laced tightly, so I let out the laces and placed the case across Jack's back as he stood beside me. The proprietor asked, "What are you fixing to do with those?"

I said, "I've got an idea in the back of my mind. We are going to try to teach Jack to pack small items between Gatlinburg and the camp and let him earn a part of his living. If we can teach him to pack supplies, that will help some. If we can train him to leave the top of the mountain and go to the store and bring back supplies by himself, we will have accomplished a great deal. This will save the Conservation Association and me a lot of money because I am having to pay four cents a pound for things delivered there."

The proprietor thought this was a smart idea. After paying two dollars for the officer's map case and briefcase, picking up my sheepskin coat and a few carpenter's tools we needed, we left the store and drove to Depot Street to a harness maker who previously had done leather work for me. I took the dog on a chain from the car, picked up the map case and briefcase, and entered the store. We walked to the rear where the harness maker was at work. He asked, "What is that across your arm, Paul?" I told him.

I said, "I'd like for you to make a bellyband and breast strap on this case and fit it to the dog." He looked at Jack and asked if the dog would bite.

I said, "Reach over and pet him on the head. He won't bite except upon my command, and I'm not going to do that."

I placed the case across the dog's shoulders and back after the man had petted Jack. The dog was docile. We found that, for the case to hang comfortably on him, I would have to let the rawhide laces out a little more. After doing this, the harness maker got down on his hands and knees to take measurements, penciling them on a scratch pad. I stood with my hand on Jack's head, and he stood perfectly still. Measurements made, the harness maker proceeded to select a long piece of cow leather, heavy yet soft. This he cut into strips about an inch and three-quarters wide.

He told me, "If this dog is going to work on the mountain, these straps must be heavy, Paul, but soft and pliable." I agreed. Within half an hour he had sewn the breast band and the buckled bellyband, on which he put a strong buckle, with a flap beneath the buckle that could be tucked underneath. This would make the pockets more comfortable for the dog to carry. He asked about a tail strap. I said that, since the dog would be packing uphill only, not downhill, I did not think a tail strap would be necessary. If I found otherwise, I'd come back. We put saddle pockets on the dog and tried to pull them off. They would not dislodge. I paid the harness maker for his work, left the saddle pockets on Jack, and returned to my car.

I drove to Mother's and picked up a few clean clothes and left some dirty ones to be laundered. Mother did not think too much of teaching the dog to pack. She said, "You can't do it. You might teach him to pack, but I don't believe that you can teach him to leave you and go to the store in Gatlinburg. Let Mr. Ogle pack up his supplies and then head him back up the mountain. I just don't believe that you are going to be able to teach him that." So I told Mother what we had done, that we had accompanied Smoky Jack down from the top of the mountain to the store and returned, and that he had whipped two packs of dogs and made the trip several times, crossing the stream on footlogs and wading the stream.

Smoky Jack and I drove back to Gatlinburg, where we stopped at the store. I thought it best to have Charlie pack the new saddle pockets with a few boxes of candy and some oranges and lemons to take up the additional space in the pockets, equalizing the weight of each pocket. Then I asked Charlie to strap them onto the dog himself and take Jack outside and give him the command to come to me. I had slipped out the back door and was standing near my car, so the dog did not have far to go to find me. He came readily and seemed happy. I took the saddle pockets off and we drove to the Orchard.

At the Orchard, I packed my supplies, put the loaded saddle pockets back on Jack, and tied my sheepskin coat securely to the top of the pack with leather thongs. The coat was not heavy, about five or six pounds, but this would give the dog a feeling of bulk weight. He could not brush against trees, because if he did, he would be knocked down or to one side. He would have to get accustomed to this way of packing. This was the only time anything was ever strapped or tied to the top of his pack.

During our hike up the mountain, we rested at Rainbow Falls and again at Last Water, where I took the pockets off to rest the dog. I had noticed on this first packing trip that Jack did not try to shake his saddle pockets off, nor did he seen to want to. I think he knew he had a duty to perform. Once or twice Smoky Jack did strike trees with his pack, and he knocked himself backward or sideways, but he righted himself and went on as if nothing had happened. He soon learned that he would have to stay in the middle of the trail. He led me all the way up, but this time he did not leap the stream. He waded it. Whenever I was packing up the mountain after the first few times, I had two places of rest, one at the top of Rainbow Falls and the other where the trail left the creek for the last time. When Jack and I were packing together, we always rested at these two places so he could stretch a little after I removed his pockets. Sometimes he had to run around a little and drink some water, but when I called to him he never hesitated in returning to me. He stood patiently as I readjusted and fastened his saddle pockets. I would usually rinse my mouth out with water at these rests. I had earlier realized that too much water would quickly wind a person. The body dehydrates from this type exertion. The evening was cool after we reached camp, so I needed the sheepskin coat for warmth as I made fire patrol. We arrived in camp, four miles above the Orchard, about fifteen minutes before sundown.

The boys and the camp guests were preparing the evening meal, but they commented on the saddle pocket-carrying dog when they saw us.

We did not come back down the mountain until the following day. I had Earnest drive us from the Orchard to Gatlinburg. Jack had on his empty saddle pockets which he carried very easily. Once in a great while, they had a tendency to ride his shoulders a little high. At those times, he would turn around so that his front legs were higher than his rear and shake the saddle pockets back into a more comfortable position. We did not take the saddle pockets off when we neared the car for the ride to the store. This time I asked Jack to bark at the door. When Charlie opened the door for the dog, we went in. Mr. Ogle took the saddle pockets off the dog and found a penciled note in them. Jack watched him intently. Charlie read the note and packed the bags, weighing them separately to make each of them about the same weight. Meantime, I left the store by the rear door and walked up the road some distance but not out of sight of the store. When the saddle pockets were fastened to the dog, Charlie brought him outside and gave him the command "Go to Paul! Go to Paul!"

Jack turned around and started up the road, saw me, and tried to run. He found it uncomfortable so slowed to a walk. When he reached me he wagged his tail, looked up into my face, and led the way to the Orchard. We walked by the two houses on the old road up Le Conte Creek, but the dogs there did not challenge us. At the lower house, the dogs were in their front yards and barked just a little. At the upper house, the mongrel who had taken a good whipping a few days before came to the gate and barked at us. Jack gave him a warning growl and the dog retreated quickly to the safety of his companions. We walked on up to the Orchard, where Earnest had bought other supplies and food from the store after Smoky Jack and I had gone. He left the car there and walked the two miles to his father's home on Sugarland Mountain.

I took off the saddle pockets to rest Jack and went about packing supplies into my own packsack. As I was doing this, the dog was running around. The next thing I knew he was chasing barnyard fowl. He attacked a chicken and killed it. I thought, *how strange that he would do such a thing.* I went over to the farmhouse and paid the lady of the house. I gave her fifty cents for the chicken and handed the chicken to her with my apology. I scolded Jack and made him stay close as I continued my packing. When I had finished, I strapped the saddle pockets on the dog, swung my own pack on my back, and made Jack lead the way up the mountain.

We made good time going up. Jack was learning quickly how to carry his load. The dog had a little difficulty in getting across the large log with the notches cut in it. I did not speak to him as we approached it but wondered how he would get over it this time. He stopped just before coming to it and studied the notches. Then he sped up, placed his left front foot and right rear foot in the second notch, missing the first one altogether, and with his next spring was on top of the log. He steadied himself there for a moment before figuring out how he was going to get off. I waited until Jack had planned his move and was back on the trail. He had learned how to get across the log without slipping.

We passed two groups of hikers going up the mountain, one group below the waterfalls and the other above. They stood aside as we passed. I spoke to the few whom I knew and told them that I was trying to teach the dog to pack supplies by himself. A youngster in one group reached out his hand to pet the dog and Jack growled at him. The boy quickly withdrew his hand. We passed the group, the dog leading. At the falls I noticed that Smoky Jack, in order to maintain his footing, sometimes took hold of rhododendron branches with his teeth to keep from slipping backward on the trail. I saw we would have to do some work on the trail here.

About a mile above the falls, we caught up with the other group hiking to the camp. All of these hikers were adults. As we approached, walking much faster than they, one man stood in the middle of the trail and would not let the dog pass. Jack stopped abruptly and growled at him. I was close behind and asked the fellow to step aside so the dog could proceed. He said, "Paul, I have petted Smoky Jack before. What is the matter with him?"

My reply was, "You have never petted him when he had his saddle pockets on. He realizes that he is working now and has something to protect. Please stand aside and let him get by." The man did.

We hiked on up the mountain and arrived well in advance of the two parties following. When I took the saddle pockets off Jack, I gave him a couple of dog biscuits which he seemed to relish. After eating, he went to the spring where he had his own drinking area. Then he took to the woods for a good run.

Earnest Ogle came back into camp early Monday morning. Lavater had left the evening before for his two-day vacation. On Tuesday I asked Earnest if he would walk Jack to Gatlinburg, have him bark at the door of the store for Charlie to admit him, and go through the same procedure of packing the saddle pockets. There were already plenty of supplies at the Orchard to be transported into camp so Earnest would not have to pack them from the store. About five hours after they left camp, they returned. Earnest told me that everything went smoothly, except for one thing. The dog had barked to be let into the store. Charlie had taken the saddle pockets off, read the enclosed note, packed the pockets with equal weight, and strapped them back on the dog. He then took him outside and said, "Go to Paul." Earnest had done the same thing that I had done earlier and started up the trail. Jack caught up with him, passed him, and led the way. At the Orchard, while Earnest was preparing his pack, he rested the dog. Jack killed another chicken in this liberty time. Earnest had to pay the farmwife another fifty cents, the same as she had charged me. He led the dog back to the barn where we kept our supplies. He chained him there for the few minutes it took to finish loading his pack. He put the saddle pockets back on the dog and started up the mountain. Earnest knew that I would reimburse him for the payment of the chicken, but I could not understand why Jack had suddenly started killing chickens.

I weighed Smoky Jack's saddle pockets. In them were twenty-five pounds. I had made up my mind that I would never pack him with more than thirty pounds. I thought that was about a proportionate amount for him to carry for his body weight of ninety pounds. From what I had read and heard, a domestic animal used in packing should never have to carry more than one-third of his body weight. (It is a little different proposition for a man. He carries the weight from his shoulders and can comfortably transport heavier loads.)

Not too many days after this trip up the mountain with Earnest, Will Ramsey showed up in camp with his rifle and several squirrels he had killed. He had traveled the short way from his home across Scratch Britches Ridge and had entered the Le Conte Creek Trail quite a distance above the Orchard. He told us he did not have guide work to do, so just decided to come up, hunting on the way, to spend the night and help us with improvements around camp. Will was a fast hiker or walker, one of the fastest I have ever known. I was complimented when he told my father one day in September, after he arrived in Gatlinburg, "That son of yours, Reverend Adams, has the 'mountainist' legs I have ever seen on an outsider. He can outwalk every one of us who have been born and raised in these mountains."

After breakfast the next morning, I asked Will if he would take the dog to the store with him, see that he was packed according to procedure, then head him back in our direction. Will said he would be glad to do this. I strapped the saddle pockets on the dog and gave him orders to go to the store. He went down the trail some distance, stopped, and found Will close behind. Will stopped, too, and I had to holler at the dog, "Go to the store, Jack. Store!" Reluctantly he turned around and led Will down the mountain. About four and a half hours after this, the dog reappeared in camp.

I heard about the experience the next day when Will came into camp leading some hikers. The dog had barked when they got to the store's door. Charlie let him in, took the saddle pockets off, opened them, read the note, packed the supplies I had ordered along with my mail, strapped the saddle pockets back on the dog, led him outside, and told him to return to me. The dog started up the road but did not go far. Perhaps he expected Will up there someplace around the curve, but he wasn't there—he was following. Will commanded the dog, "Go to Paul—go to Paul!" After the second command from Will, he started up the old road. Will told me that he had difficulty staying a fair distance behind Jack. The dog had used one footlog on this trip. He fell off of it but had righted himself. The stream was fortunately shallow.

Will followed Jack some distance above the Orchard, then left the trail after the dog was completely out of sight. Will rested before taking the shortcut to his home. I asked Will if the dog had paid any attention to barnyard fowl. Will said Jack was trotting as he reached the barn area and went right on past without the least hesitation.

A few days later, I sent Earnest to the store with the dog. He had practically the same experience with Jack. Upon reaching the Orchard, Earnest turned west at the barn and went to his parents' home for the weekend. Jack reached camp about four and a half hours after he had left. He came to me and gave a low bark, as if to say, "I'm here—take my saddle pockets off." I praised the dog, took off the saddle pockets, and gave him two dog biscuits. He went to the spring and drank water from his favorite spot. He watched me for a while and I talked to him. He then went romping in the woods.

I thought Jack had learned his first lesson. Now, could I teach him to go to the store without anyone accompanying him? Could the dog be taught? Would he leave me in camp and make the trip down the mountain to the store and return by himself? These were questions that I turned over in my mind for a few days. All I could do was to try him. My friends and I had spoken in the dog's presence of Ogle's store as THE STORE. We wanted him to be familiar with that name. Probably every native in Gatlinburg and residents of houses along the roads over which he traveled knew that we were trying to train him to make these trips alone down and up the mountain.

I waited until a Tuesday morning to try this second lesson. Lavater and Earnest were in camp. In the presence of the dog, I wrote a note on a piece of white paper and tucked it into one side of the saddle pockets, fastened the pockets, and strapped them to the dog's back. I led him to the perimeter of the camp yard and said to him, "Go to the store—*go to the store.*" He turned and started, went about fifty yards and stopped, then turned around to see if I was following. I spoke in a strong, commanding voice to get his full attention: "Jack! Go to the store." He turned around (reluctantly, I thought) and headed downhill. I sent Earnest after him when he had been gone about fifteen minutes. When Earnest came back into camp about half an hour later, he told me that he had not seen the dog at all, but he had found footprints in several places in soft earth. We believed he had followed my command and gone as instructed.

About an hour and a half later, some hikers came into camp. One of them said, "We met your dog, Paul, headed down the mountain. We stepped off the trail to let him by. He was hell-bent for someplace." I found out from them that they met the dog below the waterfall. They also told me that they had read in newspapers and had heard from mutual friends what I was trying to do. They did not realize until we told them that this was his first trip by himself.

About four hours after sending him to the store, Jack came back loaded with nails and lemons (for lemonade which we sold to hikers who preferred this to coffee or other drinks). Earnest, who was closest to the storage bins when Smoky Jack returned to camp, petted the dog, took off his saddle pockets, and gave him a couple of dog biscuits. Instead of eating them, however, Jack came to me while I was working above the campsite. His attitude seemed to be, "I've been taught to come to you, not Earnest, and here I am." I hollered down to Earnest and asked him if he had given the dog a couple of dog biscuits and he yelled back that he had, but that Jack had refused to eat them. So I walked down into camp, picked up the biscuits, and offered them to Jack. He ate then and went to the spring for a drink of water. He returned to the camp and followed me back up into the area where the present campground is, watched me for a little while as I worked, and then went wandering through the woods by himself.

Smoky Jack had learned what I hoped he would—to carry supplies without being accompanied and only on command from me. This made me happy for, from now on, I knew I could send him to the store whenever I wished.

I talked to Charlie a few days later. He told me that Jack had come to the store and barked to be let in. Charlie packed the supplies which I had ordered in the note, took the dog outside, and ordered him to return to me. Jack was seen following instructions from that end, came on up the old road, past the Orchard, and on to camp.

I was satisfied. I did not think that I would ever be without a lightweight packer again. I did send the dog along with the boys when heavier loads had to be brought up the mountain, and many times he went with me to do the same thing. But his trips were always different. We rode from the Orchard to the store in my car, which saved us considerable time.

Jack seemed to prefer me to anyone else and, of course, I was his master. I think he realized that fact. In all the many trips Jack made alone down the mountain and back, I never sent him unless I knew I myself could get down and back. I never sent him down in the winter when there was too much snow on the mountain. When snow became deep, we were stranded up there alone.

I sent Jack to the store every day for more than a week, one trip a day, for his dog biscuits. Charlie and I placed them in small packages of fifteen pounds each in heavy paper sacks. He never attempted to eat anything which had been packed. In fact, he could not get to it without first getting rid of those saddle pockets. This he never tried to do. The flaps of the saddle pockets were securely tied with rawhide straps.

I remember one Wednesday in September when I sent him to the store. Four hours passed by and no dog. Five hours passed, still no Smoky Jack. I became worried. Lavater Whaley was with me and we were rolling logs to the new cabin we were building for that winter's habitation. After five and a half hours had passed, Jack had not returned.

"Lavater," I said, "I'm worried. Perhaps the dog made a misstep in the rock bar and is struggling with a broken leg to reach the top of the mountain. Perhaps he has gotten himself lodged and can't move." I could not bear to see any living creature with pain. I told Lavater that, if the dog was hurt, I would try to carry him down to the Orchard and from there to Knoxville for medical treatment. I told Lavater not to look for me back in camp until the following day. I hurriedly walked down to a point about half a mile below the campsite, just a little below where the camp trail ran into the original one, and there was Jack, walking toward me. I stopped and waited for him to reach me. There was nothing wrong with him. I took his saddle pockets off and let him rest for five minutes before putting them back on. I did not want him to get the idea that he might be met along the trail and that we would carry his pockets for him. He led the way into camp.

FIRST LOG CABIN BUILT ON MOUNT LE CONTE, WINTER OF 1925–26. PAUL J. ADAMS
PHOTOGRAPH COLLECTION. UNIVERSITY OF TENNESSEE, KNOXVILLE LIBRARIES.

A few days later, I was in the store and asked if Charlie knew why
Jack was late returning to camp. Charlie laughed and told me that when
Jack arrived at the store, he was not there. He said, "I go to Knoxville
about every other Wednesday to pick up produce for the store. No one
around here could get close to Jack. No one could take those pockets off
him. Even Dad, who has petted the dog many times, could not get near
him. Everyone was afraid that they would be bitten and this would cause
trouble." Someone suggested maybe Will Ramsey was at home. They
called one of the two taxi drivers in Gatlinburg and told him about the
situation. He was asked to find Will Ramsey and bring him to the store
because it was known that Will could handle the dog.

Will was plowing in a field when the taxi driver found him. Will had
to unhitch his horse and put it in the barn lot before going to the store.

Will was able to take the saddle pockets off the dog. He read the note inside, packed the supplies, and sent Jack back up the mountain. That explained the delay.

A few days later, I met the helpful taxi driver. He told me, "Paul, you owe me a dollar."

"What for?" I asked. He told me that he thought that it was worth a dollar to have found Will Ramsey a few days before. I agreed, "Yeah, I think it's worth a dollar." I paid him. After that, I never sent Smoky Jack down to the store on Wednesdays.

One day in late November stands out in my memory. We had been by ourselves for several days, and I knew that Mother had sent fresh clothes for me to Gatlinburg in care of the Mountain View Hotel. Charlie Ogle always put my mail in Jack's saddle pockets, but I wanted to go to town. I wanted to take a hot bath, change clothes, and eat a good meal prepared by someone else. While I was getting ready for the trip down, I threw Jack's saddle pockets and my pack outside the door of the shack. Smoky Jack was restless this particular morning. I think he realized that we were going down when I placed the bags outside, so he stuck near me. In the preparation of the camp for the hike, I stumbled over the packsacks. I put Jack's on him to get it out of the way. He stood around as I went to the tent and tied down the flaps, came back to the shack and cleaned out the drum heater, laid a fresh fire which would be lit upon our return, then shut the door of the shack. I put on my packsack and looked around for Jack. He wasn't there. I called him. He did not answer nor come to me. I began to suspect that because I had put the saddle pockets on Jack, he thought I meant for him to go alone to the store. I had thought the dog would stick around and see what else was going to happen. Evidently he had not. I called him for two or three minutes. Still no dog.

I hurried down the trail hoping to overtake him. At the first creek crossing, I saw his fresh footprints plainly in the clay bank and knew that he was ahead of me. I hurried on. At several other creek crossings, I saw his fresh footprints. When I came to the top of Rainbow Falls, I did not go by trail across the stream but hurried to the brink of the precipice. There, far below, I saw Jack headed downhill. It took several loud calls before he heard my voice above the roar of the falls. He stopped, turned around, and looked up at me. I knew he had seen me because he wagged his tail. I called loudly for him to stay. I returned to the trail, crossed the stream, went down the bluff, and caught up with him.

After that experience, I never put Jack's saddle pockets on him until I was ready to put on my own packsack.

CHAPTER SIX

Chicken Attached to Collar

In June of 1966, I attended a weaving seminar at the Pi Beta Phi Settlement School[21] in Gatlinburg. I was greeted by a lady whom I had nearly forgotten. She exclaimed, "Paul Adams!" Surprised, I turned to see who used my name in that tone. It was Miss Winogene Redding of Pigeon Forge, a weaving teacher connected with the school. She invited me to sit down beside her and we reminisced for quite a while. It was a most pleasant chat.

Miss Redding had come to the Pi Beta Phi Settlement School in 1925 to teach weaving to mountain people. Many of those she taught lived

---

21. Pi Beta Phi Settlement School, founded in 1912 by the Pi Beta Phi Fraternity for Women, was established as an outreach effort to bring education to the mountain community of Gatlinburg. The school soon expanded its mission to encompass craft education and marketing, including weaving, under the auspices of Winogene Redding.

in remote areas. She usually rode on horseback to their homes and she had been on horseback the first time I had met her. I remember that first meeting, and it is almost as vivid as if it had happened yesterday.

I earlier mentioned that Smoky Jack sometimes killed a chicken at the upper Cherokee Orchard farmhouse near the storage barn. I finally broke him of that bad habit, although for a long time there appeared to be no way to do so. He always attacked and killed just one chicken, not two or three. Jack would kill a chicken whether he was with me, alone, or with one of my helpers. Chickens were then valued at about fifty cents each. I gave many half-dollars to the farmer's wife who lived there!

One day in late August, Jack and I had been to Gatlinburg for supplies in my Model T Ford and had returned to the Orchard. While I was packing his saddle pockets and my pack, I heard the squawking of chickens. When I looked around, Jack was gone! I ran toward the racket. Chickens were half-running, half-flying to get out of the "killer's" way. I hollered at Jack. He paid no attention to me. Before my and everyone's eyes, he caught a hen by the neck in mid-air, crushed the neck and head, and laid it down. Then he sheepishly turned and came to me. I did not say one word to him but walked over to the lady of the house, pulled out my pocketbook, and paid her fifty cents. One of her children had retrieved the dead fowl and carried it to the porch. The lady told me that about the only time the family had chicken was when my dog killed one. She also told me that whenever he passed the house going to the store in Gatlinburg, or upon his return trip by himself to the top of the mountain, he never even looked at the chickens. This seemed strange to me. I asked her if she had a very strong piece of small rope that I could have. One of her children, realizing what I had in mind, asked me if a piece of bailing wire would not be better. I told him I thought maybe it would, so he fetched a piece of wire about three feet long.

Taking the broad, brass-studded collar off the dog, I proceeded to wire the chicken to the outside of it and then replaced the collar around Jack's neck. He wore his "trophy" for about two weeks. I had to secure that chicken to his collar many times. He wore it continuously until there was nothing much left of the chicken. He was not allowed to go into the tent on top of the mountain nor was he allowed to enter my shack. I had little to say to him during this punishment. He would scratch at his collar and try to dislodge this terrible thing around his neck. The boys and I would holler at him when we caught him doing it and make him stop. I was determined that the dead chicken would stay on Jack's collar.

I can only guess whether he missed being sent to the store by himself during this period. He did make several trips with one of us along, and it was on one of those occasions that I met Miss Redding. I had heard of her and her work. She had heard of me and of the big dog that packed supplies to the top of the mountain, so we knew of each other before we finally met.

I had left the Ogle store without taking the saddle pockets off Jack. I walked toward the Mountain View Hotel, where I expected to eat dinner before returning to the top of the mountain. Jack trotted beside me. As we approached the main entrance of the school grounds, I saw Miss Redding, on horseback, coming our way. I sidestepped to give the horse the right-of-way. I had no intention of stopping, having never been introduced to her. I would not have spoken more than the word "howdy," as was the custom of all mountaineers when they met someone. I did not, however, get this salutation out of my mouth. Miss Redding reined in her horse and stopped in the middle of the road. She called my name and berated me for treating a dumb animal so cruelly. The shock of being spoken to in that tone of voice made me stop. For a few seconds, I was so dumbfounded that I could not have spoken even if I had wanted to. When she finally paused, I told her about Smoky Jack killing chickens and explained why the half-rotten chicken was around his neck. She had seen the dog many times on his way to the store or on the return trip and had heard of the dog killing chickens at the Orchard. After I explained the situation, she agreed with me that this ought to cure the dog of killing chickens. But she asked me not to treat him this way again, even if the experience did not cure him. We parted, she going to the Pi Beta Phi School, and Smoky Jack and I again heading for the hotel.

I chained the dog to a fencepost near the hotel and carried his saddle pockets across my arm to the porch. After I had washed for dinner, I sat on the porch with other guests. Several of those present asked me what was around the dog's neck that "smelled." I had to again explain the situation. Before allowing Jack to accompany me back to the top of the mountain that day, I reattached the dangling chicken legs and wings and decided this would be the last time. After another week, the chicken was completely deteriorated, so I took the bailing wire off the collar.

Following that experience, Jack never paid any attention to chickens, not even to let them know he was near. The chickens and ducks at the Orchard were safe, but they continued to give Jack plenty of room when he made his appearance. Even after Jack went to Alpine[22] to live, we could not "sic" him on the neighbor's chickens which sometimes came into our garden. We had to chase them away. The same thing happened when he moved with my wife and me to Crab Orchard,[23] where he lived out his remaining days.

He never again chased a chicken.

---

22. Alpine is a small community in Overton County, Tennessee, where Adams moved with his family in 1928. It is home to the Alpine Institute.

23. Crab Orchard is a town in Cumberland County, Tennessee.

CHAPTER SEVEN

Attacks on People

During the first few weeks after I purchased Smoky Jack, he was slow to make friends with people. He became a sociable animal and made many friends later in life and at times he lived with my parents. But most persons were afraid of him because of his size and the reputation of his breed. Many shepherds were used exclusively in police work and many of them were not allowed to have liberty. They were always chained or confined to small running yards and pens. Perhaps that lack of freedom toughened the dispositions of such shepherds. I have never owned a dog I had to keep confined and I certainly was not going to allow Smoky Jack to suffer such an indignity.

During his later years, when I would arrive home for a few days or weeks, Smoky Jack and I were almost inseparable. Sometimes he would follow me into church on Sundays, although he was told to stay home. He would pick up my scent and follow me to the church, stand for a moment in the back, then walk over to me. I would point my finger to the floor, where he knew he was supposed to lie down and stay until church services were over. I would reach down and pet his head and the dog seemed satisfied to lie there at my feet. I would never have to issue commands at these times nor interrupt my father while he was delivering his sermon. My father would, of course, see the dog first because he was facing his parishioners, while the audience was facing the rostrum in front of the door. When Father would faintly smile while delivering his sermon, I knew it was because of Jack. The dog always came directly to me, so I usually sat at the end of a row of seats in the church. He did not have to walk by others in the same pew when he came to me. When the closing song was sung and the benediction given, he would still be lying on the floor. He would not rise until I called him. The only time Jack went into the church was when I was at home. When I was away, he would wait in the yard near the church. When the services were over and my parents started home, Jack would run to meet them and accompany them back to the manse.

When I had to go to a local meeting in Alpine, Jack would follow me. Usually, the main door of the meeting place was closed, but the dog had a way of letting me know that he was outside. He would give one very loud bark, which could be heard by everyone in the room, then he would lie down to await my coming out to walk home with him. Sometimes the chairman of the meeting would ask me to go to the door and let my dog in to lie at my feet. Everyone in the small Alpine community knew Jack and had a lot of respect for him. He was commonly known there as "Jack Adams."

I believe Jack felt his responsibility to me more when he had his saddle pockets on than when he did not. Few persons attempted to lay their hands upon him when those pockets were in place. He was all business then. He had a duty to perform and he knew it. When we were packing up the mountain together, he would pay no attention to game of any sort or to chickens in farmers' yards or to people in general.

The summer when I put Jack's saddle pockets on him to send him to the store by himself, I had worried as to whether he would return at the usual time of four and a half hours. This was particularly true when we had visitors at night. I knew the dog would attack if teased and others should have realized this, too. Once in a great while I would hear of Jack's attacking someone, but this was only if provoked by a person trying to block his way or grab at him as he passed. These provocations came mostly from boys in their teenage years who did not grasp the idea that a working animal should not be molested.

We sometimes had a few wounded hands and arms requiring first aid in camp. We had no way of knowing that the dog had attacked anyone until that person walked into camp and told us about it. Jack came into camp without showing any signs of having encountered someone on the trail. He always came in with loaded saddle pockets. One of my boys or I would remove them, give him a couple of dog biscuits, and then he would run around by himself for a while in the woods. But when those whom he had bitten came into camp with wounded hands, he would never have anything to do with them. At these times, he would stay close to my side. If that person approached a little too close to me, according to Jack's way of thinking, he would growl or snarl and let it be known that he would protect me.

On two occasions, men walked into the camp and asked for guns to shoot the dog. We laughed about it and told those fellows that, if the dog tried to bite them, it was their own fault because we were certain that they had tried to interfere with the dog's work. Once or twice I commented that some people showed less sense than a child when they tried to pet a working dog. There had been newspaper articles about the dog packing supplies from Gatlinburg to the top of Mount Le Conte. So most people knew about Jack and, if he walked up behind them, would get out of his way by stepping off the trail and letting him pass.

I remember one particular time when a young man came into camp with several companions. He had a bloody, mutilated hand. Smoky Jack was not in the camp at the time, but he had made a trip to town and back that morning. His saddle pockets had been taken off. He had been given his usual reward and had gone romping in the woods by himself. Earnest and I dressed the boy's hand and bandaged it, then he asked for a gun to kill the dog.

According to the boy's companions, the dog overtook them near the last creek crossing where the trail narrowed. While most of the boys stood aside to let the working dog by, this boy attempted to stop Jack by grabbing at his collar. The dog flinched, drew back, and growled at the boy, repeatedly warning him, "Let me pass!" The boy finally stood aside at the insistence of his companions, but he reached out to take another grab at the dog's collar as Jack passed. This time he got a hold on it. Smoky Jack, not used to such treatment, turned quickly. He caught the boy's hand and bit it hard several times. The boy, recoiling in pain, was hollering as he looked at his bleeding hand. Jack had turned and walked on up the trail.

The boy was still angry about Jack even after we had dressed the hand and he told me that when I made my night fire patrol he would kill the dog. I did not have time to reply, for Earnest and Lavater both spoke sharply to the boy. They told him in no uncertain terms that, if anything happened to this dog, they would see to it that he would never reach his home again. They meant every word. Feuds have been started in the mountains over things more minor than the killing of a dog. I did not say a word. I knew I did not have to. Nothing happened. Jack came back into camp, but for some reason he stayed close to our quarters and did not go near the tent or cooking area. I made fire patrol that night, and Smoky Jack went with me.

The following morning, as Jack went with Earnest to the spring to bring water for our quarters, this boy and his companions were also at the spring. The dog was leading. The boy, who was standing above the trail, kicked the dog very hard in the ribs. I heard a yelp of pain from the dog and wondered what had happened. I soon found out.

Earnest set his two pails down and immediately jumped the boy with his flailing fists. A fight followed. I heard, above the din of barking and cursing, the voices of other boys yelling, "Fight, fight, fight!" as they gathered around to watch.

I ran toward the spring. I knew if Smoky Jack got a hold on this boy's throat, he would rip it open. I shouted at Jack and he listened. I grabbed his collar and pulled him out of the fight. He stood beside me, breathing heavily. We stood there and watched Earnest give the boy a sound thrashing. He tried to run, but Earnest knocked him down a couple of times. Finally stepping in between them, I asked them to stop fighting. They did. The young man who had started it was completely cowed and whipped. I told all those present at the spring that this would be the last of the incident. As I led the way back into camp, Smoky Jack walked ahead of me. Twice he looked back across his shoulder into my face as if to say, "That boy had it coming to him. Why did you interrupt?"

This group stayed two days on the mountain. Smoky Jack stayed close to me and watched every movement I made as we went about our camp duties. There were two other groups in camp at the time and many comments were made about the incident. Different persons had different opinions as to how I should have handled the situation. But I knew too well that, if I had allowed the dog to fight this young man, Jack would have jumped for the boy's throat and killed him in seconds. I did not want murder committed.

I have never known Jack to attack a woman and, so far as I knew, no female ever tried to stop him. With men and boys it was a little different. Guides accompanying parties up the mountain saw to it that everyone stood aside to let the dog pass. Once or twice when Will Ramsey was with a group while Jack was packing, he would call the dog to a halt. It depended on which part of the trail they were on when they met. Jack heeded his voice because he had been taught to take instructions from Will. Will would sometimes rest the dog by taking his saddle pockets off for a few minutes and then strapping them back on. On these occasions, anyone in the party Will was guiding could pet Smoky Jack. I think the dog appreciated Will's thoughtfulness. When he came into camp after these rests, Jack was more attentive than usual to Will.

Men and boys with whom Jack had trouble along the trail, whether they were bitten or not, could not later approach the dog without his growling or snarling viciously at them. A few times I asked these individuals what they had done to the dog. Of course, they denied doing anything. But my helpers and I always knew that something had happened. Jack just would not make friends with them. He might be friendly with others in the group. He might accept food from them and bring it to one of us to examine before handing it back to him to eat. But with those people with whom he had had trouble, he would stand his ground and give off low growls and perhaps snarl. Jack never forgot such a person, even when they met later in life. He just did not have any use for these individuals. They say that an elephant "never forgets." Sometimes I believe that a dog never forgets either.

I was a charter member of the Smoky Mountains Hiking Club and, after Smoky Jack and I lived on top of Mount Le Conte, from July 1925 to May 1926, we made many hikes with the club. I would usually have Jack carry his saddle pockets. All the members of the club were well acquainted with the dog and we experienced no trouble. But when visitors went along with the club, and the dog was carrying his saddle pockets, we asked them to keep their hands off the dog. Most visitors had heard about Jack, but there were a few exceptions. The dog quickly learned that, when we were on hikes of this type, with many others along, he should stay close to me. When rest times came, and he sat on his haunches beside me, he could be petted by children and adults alike. When we reached our destination and the saddle pockets were taken off, he was friendly with everyone.

If the hike was for two or three days and we camped out at night, Jack would curl up near me to sleep. One ear was always alert for unusual sounds and he was ready to spring up to protect those with him. If someone got up to replenish a campfire to take the chill off the night, Jack would always rise to watch whoever was building up the fire. Then he would stretch a little and return to lie near me. If the club spent the night in the Hall Cabin[24] or at Spence Field Cabin[25] or even on top of Mount Le Conte, he would never sleep in the cabins. When he saw that

---

24. Hall Cabin was a hunters' lodge that straddled the state line at Derrick Knob on the main Smoky divide.

25. Spence Field Cabin refers to a herders' cabin that stood on the North Carolina side of Spence Field just west of the large spring that flows to Eagle Creek.

I was preparing to retire, he would ask to go out. He was always curled up outside the door when I arose in the morning.

When members of the Hiking Club were helping to clear the Appalachian Trail, Jack and I went on two hikes. I packed his food and small articles for myself, but I would never allow him to carry a cutting tool on the outside of his saddle pockets. I was afraid that he might make a misstep, fall, and injure himself. Since he usually led the parties on Appalachian Trail clearing expeditions, he would sometimes take off after a rabbit. If his pack was not too heavy and the woods open, he would soon bring back fresh meat.

CHAPTER EIGHT

Broken Leg

My trips down the mountain were made during the hiking and tourist season when my summer helpers were in camp. My presence was not always required to keep things running smoothly. Lavater Whaley and Earnest Ogle had known each other all their lives and I placed a lot of confidence in them. They could wait on our guests as well as me and I trusted them implicitly. I knew that, if I did not return by nightfall, one of them would make fire patrol—a duty we had to perform twice a day during fire season.

One beautiful mid-week morning, Smoky Jack and I left the camp soon after breakfast and hiked down to the Orchard. We took my car and drove on down into Gatlinburg to transact business. Around noon, I headed for the Mountain View Hotel to eat dinner before starting back for the top of the mountain. The small parking area at the hotel was crowded and I parked close to another automobile. I left Jack stretched out in the front seat, unchained him, and gave him the command to "stay" before entering the hotel.

On the hotel porch, I sat in a rocking chair to await the dinner bell. I talked with others who were waiting the call to dinner. One of them asked where Smoky Jack was, and I said he was in the car. "Would you mind calling him up here, Paul, so I can show him to my friends?"

I did not mind, so I whistled for Jack to come. He heard the whistle and we saw him stand up in the car, measure the distance to the ground, and jump. He left the car on the left-hand side and jumped a little too short. One of his front legs struck the running board. He let out a howl of pain. I left my chair and ran to him. He was coming in my direction walking on three legs, holding one front foot high. I examined the leg. The radius bone was broken. He was not going to let a little thing like a broken leg interfere with a command from me!

I did not wait for dinner. A friend helped me get Jack back into the front seat and we immediately started for Sevierville and Knoxville. I had heard of a veterinarian in Sevierville, but I had not previously dealt with him. When I stopped at his office, his advice was to shoot the dog and put him out of his misery. I thought to myself that there was something funny here since Jack continuously growled and snarled at the doctor. I had to hold the dog as the doctor examined him to keep the doctor from getting bitten. I told the doctor I would take the dog on to Knoxville to a veterinarian who had treated the dog before and who I knew could and would set the leg because he was a lover of dogs. About three weeks later, I found out why there was hatred between the dog and doctor and why the doctor had advised me to shoot Jack. The doctor had been bitten by the dog during one of his trips up the mountain while packing supplies. The doctor had tried to stop him along the trail between the Orchard and Rainbow Falls. No wonder there was animosity between them.

I drove my car very fast between Sevierville and Knoxville, knowing that the sooner we arrived there, the sooner the dog would receive relief. He was still in the front seat with me and licked the hurt place on his leg during much of the ride. Once in a while he would look up at me as if to say, "Master, my leg hurts. I wish you would do something about it."

We finally arrived in Knoxville and I drove directly to Dr. Jacobs's State Street office and stable. I told the doctor that Smoky Jack had a broken leg. He walked out to the car and helped me get the dog into his office and up on a long table. Smoky Jack recognized the veterinarian and did not offer any resistance when the doctor examined the leg. Dr. Jacobs shook a couple of pills out of a bottle, handed them to me, and asked that I force them down the dog's throat while he went to get splints and bandages. I got the pills down Jack's throat and in a few minutes he was calm.

When the doctor completed his work on the dog's leg, he said, "Paul, I don't believe that, if I were you, I'd take this dog back to the top of Mount Le Conte. Leave him here for at least two weeks, until his leg heals." So I did. We placed Jack in one of the stalls at the rear of the building and gave him a pan of fresh water. I did not think to tell the doctor that it was I who fed the dog most of the time. That was a big mistake.

I ate a late lunch in Knoxville before walking down to Colonel Chapman's office for a short visit. I told him that Jack had broken his leg in Gatlinburg that noon, that I had rushed him to Dr. Jacobs, and that he would stay there while the leg healed. Colonel Chapman told me that he would walk down and see the dog every other day or so. They knew each other. He had known Dr. Jacobs for several years and thought highly of him. After our short visit, I drove back to Cherokee Orchard and climbed the mountain that night, arriving there before the boys had gone to bed. Of course, they wanted to know where Smoky Jack was and I told them the story. It was a lonesome two weeks up there for all three of us because we had become accustomed to having the dog around.

When I returned to Knoxville to get Jack, he was not there. Dr. Jacobs was not there. A new stable man had been hired and he said he did not know about any large German shepherd police dog. I became worried.

I asked the new hired man, "Did the doctor take the dog with him when he left here?" supposing he had taken the dog with him on his rounds. The hired man said, "There hasn't been any dog at all here since I've been working. No, the doctor did not take a dog with him." I asked when the doctor was expected back and he told me there was no telling what time he would be there. I knew this was true.

I walked up State Street toward Colonel Chapman's office and dropped in for a visit. He smiled when I walked into his office and said, "Paul, Smoky Jack is out at Russell Smith's." He told me that he had visited the dog as he had promised. Jack would not eat, not for him or for the doctor. They tried to get him to eat fresh beef that they bought at the city market, but the dog turned up his nose at everything offered. After the fourth day of Jack's not eating, they decided to call Russell Smith and tell him about the circumstances.

When Russell came in the stable, Smoky Jack was so happy to see him that he nearly rebroke his leg. For his old handler, Jack ate. Russell suggested that he take the dog out to his place. Jack's old running yard was empty and the dog would have an outside pen to run in when he felt like it. He would be around other dogs—some of his old companions— and it would save Russell coming into the city twice a day to feed him.

This was good news to me. I went back to Dr. Jacobs's office and he asked me, "Paul, why didn't you tell me that your dog had been trained not to accept food from anyone except yourself? We had a terrible time with him the first four days. He'd drink water, but he wouldn't eat dog biscuits, fresh beef, or anything given to him by either myself or Colonel Chapman. The colonel suggested I call Russell Smith, and when he walked in here and went back to the stall to see Jack, the dog ate for him." He also said that, two days before, he had passed by Russell's, stopped to see the dog, and took the splints off. Jack ran around without the least sign of being crippled and was walking normally.

I paid Dr. Jacobs's bill and was about to leave when the doctor suggested I not use the dog in packing supplies for a few days until he had regained his normal strength. I went immediately to Russell Smith's to reclaim my dog. Jack was overjoyed to see me and was anxious to return with me to camp. We drove toward Gatlinburg and Cherokee Orchard, arriving there late in the afternoon.

I put a few supplies in my packsack and was about to lock the door of the supply room when Smoky Jack made a dash into the room. I wondered what was wrong with him. He went over to his saddle pockets, hanging on a nail, and pulled at them with his teeth. He seemed to ask, "Aren't you going to put these on me? Aren't you forgetting that I pack supplies?" I shook my head and tried to explain to him that it was the doctor's orders that he not be packed for a few days. He was so reluctant to leave without wearing his saddle pockets that I thought to myself, "Three or four pounds surely won't hurt you." I strapped the empty pockets on him.

Jack and I walked up the mountain together. I watched him closely as we made the climb. He did not limp. Upon arriving in camp, I took off his saddle pockets and gave him a couple of dog biscuits. He ate these, went to the spring for a drink of water, and came back into camp. He did not have his usual romp in the woods, but he seemed happy to get back to his old stomping grounds. We were glad he felt this way and we were glad to have him back. It had been lonesome for us during his absence.

CHAPTER NINE

High Trail Robbery

I am a happy-go-lucky sort of person when alone. So I whistled and sang a lot when I was in the woods, particularly when I was going downhill and not hunting. I have always been that way. I still whistle softly as I hike alone along woodland trails.

One morning in early August, after a full weekend of hikers and campers, I decided to go down the mountain with Smoky Jack for a load of food and supplies. The two of us, with our empty packs on, walked down the Rainbow Falls Trail. Jack was leading. I was whistling. We had passed the first crossing of Le Conte Creek, had gone through the large "graybacks" area between there and Rainbow Falls, and had skirted the cliff of the falls. We were near the end of the horseback trail when Jack came to a complete stop about fifty feet in front of me, gave off a low growl, and snarled. The bristles on his back rose and he pointed his nose toward a very large poplar around which the trail led. I stopped to look around and saw nothing exciting. I listened for a moment more,

CAMP ON MOUNT LE CONTE, 1925. IDENTIFIED IN THE PHOTOGRAPH ARE UNCLE MANNING (FAR LEFT STANDING), ALBERT "DUTCH" ROTH (STANDING, FOURTH FROM THE LEFT), MARSHALL OGLE (STANDING, FIFTH FROM LEFT), WILL RAMSEY (STANDING, SIXTH FROM THE LEFT), JIM THOMPSON (STANDING, SEVENTH FROM THE LEFT), BROCKWAY CROUCH (SEATED, FOURTH FROM THE LEFT), H. P. IJAMS AND ALICE IJAMS WITH THEIR FOUR CHILDREN (SEATED IN CENTER), LAVATER WHALEY (SECOND FROM RIGHT), AND PAUL ADAMS IN FRONT HOLDING AXE. SMOKY JACK IS HIDING UNDER THE TABLE. PHOTOGRAPHER IS ROBIN THOMPSON, BROTHER OF JIM. THOMPSON PHOTOGRAPH COLLECTION. MCCLUNG HISTORICAL COLLECTION.

then encouraged the dog to lead on down the trail. I figured that he had heard a snake crawling away from the path. At such times he acted in this manner. He went on hesitantly, more cautious now and his back still bristling.

As I rounded the large poplar, a man stepped out from behind it and thrust a revolver into my ribs. This happened so quickly that I did not have time to draw my own gun. This man—if it was a man and I had every indication to think so—was very shabbily dressed and his clothes were much too large. He had a false mustache across his upper lip and wore a brown wig which hung down below his shoulders. A gray hat was pulled down over his forehead, half-hiding his eyes. His face was pock-marked. I did not recognize him.

My hands dropped to my sides and, as Jack had already stopped, I spoke the word "stay." I was more afraid for the dog's safety than for mine and, by giving him this command, I knew he would be quiet. Our waylayer drew my 44-caliber colt revolver from its holster with his free hand, emptied the shells at my feet, and tucked the gun inside his belt. He then jabbed me again with his own cocked revolver. It was not a comfortable feeling. He ordered me to surrender all the money I had. I complied, taking a roll of bills out of my pants pocket and handing it to him. He told me to turn around, face up mountain, and not to follow him until a full five minutes had elapsed. I tried to recognize his gruff voice, but I could not. I felt certain that he was also disguising his voice.

The man told me he would leave my gun fifty or sixty yards down the trail. At least he was a gentleman from that standpoint. I turned and faced the top of Mount Le Conte and never once did I peek over my shoulder as the retreating man's steps faded out of hearing. I stood in this about-face position for a full five minutes, giving the fellow time enough to retreat. Then I picked up the six unspent shells from my gun and encouraged Smoky Jack to lead the way on down the trail.

When he came to my gun, which the holdup man had left about a hundred yards down the trail, the dog stopped and sniffed at it, gave a low growl, and stood beside it. I walked to the gun, picked it up, reloaded it, and stuck it back into my holster. When I was ready to go on, Smoky Jack's nose went to the ground. He ran through the woods, seemingly intent on trailing the fellow who had held us up. The forest in this area was what I would term open woods with very little undergrowth. In spots a person could see for several hundred yards. I let Smoky Jack follow the man for fifteen or twenty yards, but I called him back after not finding any shoe print which the man might have made. We kept on to Cherokee Orchard, climbed into the T-Model, and drove down to Ogle's store.

I called Charlie aside into one of the store's storage rooms and told him what had happened. He made light of the incident and told me there were men in the community who had been guilty of such actions, that these few men were more or less vagabonds, and they were, at times, trigger happy. In all probability, if I had so much as stepped backward to draw my gun, I would have been killed on the spot, Charlie said.

I mailed a short letter to Colonel Chapman telling him how much money had been taken. The morning was still young, so Smoky Jack and I filled our packs, reentered the car, and drove back to the Orchard. I parked my car beside the old apple barn and we hiked back up the mountain, arriving at the top about noon.

Besides Charlie Ogle, I told both Earnest and Lavater of the incident. Beyond this, word went no farther.

There were many more hikes down the mountain and returns to the top after we were held up the first time. On August 11, 1925, during the third Park Commission trip, I handed Colonel Chapman all the money we had collected since the holdup.

I was now more cautious going down the mountain when I carried money.

Sometimes I carried my revolver in my hand, ready for instant action if another occasion arose, until we passed the end of the horseback trail. I would reholster the gun as we neared the barn at the Orchard or came within hollering distance of a farmhouse in the upper end of the Orchard. I did not believe I would be attacked that close to the barn.

Soon after Labor Day, I decided that I would go to Ogle's store. We had quite a bit of money to take down the mountain for deposit. This time, I took all my bills and placed them in a long envelope, sealed it, and placed it in the dog's saddle pockets. Perhaps, if I were held up again, the robber would not find any money.

I carried my revolver in my hand between Rainbow Falls and the upper end of the horseback trail before reholstering it. Smoky Jack jumped a rabbit and took after it at the elevation where young apple trees had been planted. Within another hundred feet, I was held up a second time. This time there was no warning from Jack. The man who came out from behind a large shoulder-high boulder certainly had the advantage of me. He took my gun away from me, emptying it of the cartridges at my feet. Sticking the gun into his belt, he demanded money. I told the shabbily dressed man with his old hat pulled down over his eyes that I was not carrying money, that I had sent the money down the mountain on Labor Day. The fellow did not believe me. He searched my pockets and found only five dollars of personal money. This he took. Again, I had to face the top of the mountain as he retreated.

I was still facing the mountain when Jack came back with a rabbit. He dropped the rabbit at my feet, bristled, and uttered low growls. I told him to be quiet, but this did not stop his bristling. I waited for the five minutes, picked up the six unspent shells from my revolver, and we walked on down the trail to where the robber had left my gun. This time the dog wanted to pick up the trail which led toward Le Conte Creek instead of in the direction of Scratch Britches Ridge. Again, we did not attempt to follow him.

I told the Orchard workers about the robbery and asked if they had seen someone sneaking through the woods. The only people they had seen were hikers who parked in the Orchard before hiking up the mountain. I gave the young rabbit to the farm housewife after she told me that one of her children would dress it for their dinner.

Smoky Jack and I climbed into my car and drove on down to the store. Again I called Charlie aside, took the sealed envelope out of Jack's saddle pockets, opened it, and counted the money. Charlie gave me a receipt. He thought this was a clever idea, to let the dog carry the money, and assured me he would not tell anyone about it. Whoever would think of looking into a dog's saddle pockets for money?

I am confident that whoever it was who had robbed us once, and attempted it the second time, knew when large parties came to the top of the mountain for an extended stay. He must have watched or heard of such parties and he knew when groups spent more than one night there. He had sense enough to realize that, after they left the area, there was some money left behind. I probably had it on my person or had it hidden someplace around the camp.

We did have a large crowd up there the 10th, 11th, and 12th of October 1925. Although I needed some supplies after this, I put off for a few days my trip down to Ogle's store. The snow which had fallen on the 10th of the month had melted. The ground was wet.

I knew we would have to go soon to Gatlinburg to get flour, eggs, spikes, and nails and to start Smoky Jack packing food in for the winter. I had asked Charlie earlier to get a hundred and fifty pounds of crumbled dog food, scraps of dog biscuits—sacked and, of course, slightly cheaper than the whole biscuit. We would put these into fifteen-pound sacks to place in the dog's saddle pockets, two at a time, and let him bring these to camp. Charlie had put a note into the dog's saddle pockets telling me that they were at his store and I knew that it would be up to me to help pack them in sacks. Mother had written me a postal card telling me that she had sent some fresh clothes for me in care of the Mountain View Hotel.

At dusk one night, I had just finished washing my dishes and entered our shack to start a fire in the drum heater to take off the evening chill. In a few minutes, Smoky Jack followed me in, then gave off a low growl. He snarled and his bristles rose. I followed him outside. He advanced a little past the cooking fire in the direction of the spring and stood his ground. Thinking that maybe it was a bear, I yelled a couple of times. After hearing nothing, and receiving no reply, I stepped back into the shack and strapped on my revolver. I picked up a flashlight with a powerful beam and went back outside. The dog was at my heels and then ran ahead of me just a few feet but this time in a different direction. Although I had been working hard all day, I was not too tired to realize that we had an intruder! I did not want to hiss at the dog since he could have been shot if someone was behind a tree. There was still a little light but not enough for me to see more than fifty or sixty feet. I decided to build a fire between the shack and the half-built cabin to throw more light in the area. I was not about to be rushed and shot.

I ordered Jack to lie down. Being black, he could not plainly be seen from any great distance. I tried to keep out of sight as much as possible but did have to keep that fire going. The dog changed positions often and pointed in the direction of large trees around the perimeter of the camp area, still growling and bristling. I was certain it was no bear out there but a man, intent upon robbing us in a bold way. He did not dare shoot at me for fear of being attacked by the dog. He did not dare shoot at the dog either, for the dog remained in his lying-down position at least thirty feet from the fire. When he would change to a new position to point in another direction, he would crawl to it instead of getting up and walking. He continually pointed toward the large trees on the edge of the camp yard.

Round and round that fellow went that evening as Jack's actions indicated. The fellow must have been cold, watching us from behind one tree and then another, since the temperature was near freezing. About two hours after Smoky Jack had first warned me, his last "point" was near the trail leading out of the camp yard toward the Rainbow Falls Trail. I replenished the fire. I noticed that the dog's bristles were back to normal. After a few moments, his growling and snarling stopped. He looked over at me and I asked him to come to me. He did.

Feeling a little easier now, I lit the fire in the drum heater to warm the shack, preparatory to going to bed, and then returned outside to stand beside Jack. He showed no sign that the prowler was still around. I slept very lightly that night, waking every now and then to listen. I left a lantern burning all night in the living room. I left the door ajar to the shack. If Jack had to awaken me, he could come in and do so without barking. He had been trained to awaken a sleeping master by running his cold nose down the back of the neck.

Once when a bear had passed through camp, he awakened me in this manner. By the time I had slipped my britches on, grabbed my revolver, and gone outside the shack, we heard the bear down at the latrines. I plainly saw in the camp yard the bear's large tracks. We made no attempt to go after the animal, for we were not there to kill bears. I went to bed. The next morning we found that the bear had cleaned out both latrines before leaving the area.

After breakfast the next morning, Smoky Jack and I examined the ground behind some large trees where our most recent intruder had stood. We found many well-defined tracks of shoe prints where he had stood watching our movements. These prints had a definite outline. I got a piece of heavy paper and a ruler and pencil to measure and draw a rough sketch of the design of the track. The toe of the footprint had a small steel plate on it, while the heel had a definite steel cross and was outlined by another steel plate. I made very careful measurements and with a pair of scissors cut an outline of the shoe. I folded this paper and put it in my shirt pocket, thinking that I might later be able to identify the tracks.

Smoky Jack, who was standing nearby, gave a very low growl and bristled. I grabbed my gun and cocked it, then turned around to see Will Ramsey walking up the trail by himself. Jack also saw him and his bristles fell and his attitude changed from that of warning to friendliness. Will spotted us and came over to see what we were doing. I reholstered my revolver. He had not seen us for several days, so he had walked up to find out how we were getting along. He brought some freshly killed squirrels. He and I discussed the problem of the intruder. He could not identify the shoe prints. He told me that perhaps the man had changed shoes down the trail. We both knew that this was a possibility. I told Will then about being held up twice before and of the amounts of money taken.

He said that Colonel Chapman had told him about one incident and asked him to keep it quiet but he was to check on me every now and then and keep his ears and eyes open. Will spent most of the day with us. About the middle of the afternoon, Will left the camp, allowing time to be home by nightfall. He knew I possessed a 45-90 rifle and told me that it might be a good idea for me to bring it to camp from Knoxville because its bullets would penetrate and go through any tree around camp. He would let it be known around Gatlinburg that we had an intruder.

I thought it best to wait for a couple of days before going to Gatlinburg after Will had paid me that visit. On the third morning, I again

placed the money we had for deposit in the dog's saddle pockets and we started down the trail. We arrived at the Orchard in good condition, having no trouble at all going down the mountain. We drove to the store, but before entering I took the dog's saddle pockets off, gave him the order to lie down, and dropped his lead chain beside him. I gave him the order to "stay."

I carried Jack's saddle pockets across my arm to the store. There were several men standing outside talking among themselves. I spoke to all of them and said more than "howdy" to some. They had heard of the attempted holdup and one of them asked me if I was not scared. I told him, "Hell, yes, I was scared! I would have shot anyone there that night!" They told me they probably would have acted the same but they could not figure out who around Gatlinburg would try such a thing. Most of those around town were our friends.

I had not been in the store more than five minutes when we heard Smoky Jack's chain rattle as it was dragged behind him. At the same time, he gave a loud bark followed by a snarl. I rushed out of the store to see what was taking place, closely followed by Charlie and others in the store. Smoky Jack had a man backed up against the side of the store, his front feet on the man's shoulders, with the man pinned against the side of the building. Charlie saw the situation and whispered to me, "There is your man, Paul."

The man whom Jack had captured had his hands on his exposed neck, trying to protect it. The dog was snarling with open mouth and his bristles were raised high on his back. I walked to within ten feet of the man and dog. The man was very nervous. He was not wearing clothes too large for him or a false mustache and long wig. He begged me to make the dog get down but I told him that I would not "call off" Jack until he had answered a few questions.

Charlie said, "Paul, make the man show you the bottom of his shoe."

The man asked why I should ask such a question, and I said, "Well, we had a visitor on top of the mountain a few nights ago. I am pretty sure that he came up there to rob and perhaps kill me and Jack." I went on to say that the next morning I had found many footprints behind some of the larger trees around the camp, that the tracks had been seen by another person, and that I wanted to examine the soles of his shoes.

He said, "No, I will not show them to you."

I asked him if he wanted me to give the dog the "attack" command.

"No! Make the dog get down. I haven't done anything to you or him to make him attack me."

Again, I asked him to show me the soles of his shoes. The man complied very reluctantly and brought one of his shoes up above the knee of the other leg. I examined the shoe closely. It appeared to me that it was the same imprint I had found at the campsite. I reached into my shirt pocket, took out the rough sketch I had been carrying, and placed it against the shoe. My drawing fit exactly against the steel plate in the toe of the shoe and the heel markings. Everyone around us saw it. Then I ordered Jack to get down. He did, but he made no attempt to retreat, standing there in front of the man with his bristles still up and snarling.

I asked the man if he had been the intruder on top of the mountain a few nights before. He denied it, of course. Then I asked him why the dog had taken such an interest in him. The man became white as a sheet. I told him that if he or any other man tried such a trick again I would throw hand grenades in the general direction in which the dog pointed. I was considered a fairly good underhand thrower of such objects. I also said I was bringing from my home in Knoxville a 45–90 rifle, which would penetrate any tree up on the mountain.

Thank goodness, this man was not a resident of Gatlinburg. He lived some distance away, up on Sugarlands near the Fighting Creek Gap.

One of my friends, who had been with me many times in the mountains and saw the confrontation, told me that I had a perfectly good court case with all the witnesses. He said that he would be willing to testify on our behalf, but I told him that any court proceedings in Sevierville would not be believed by any jury solely on my testimony and particularly not the testimony of a dog. I promised to make a report to Colonel Chapman about it but I was sure he would not want to press charges.

CHAPTER 10

Huggins Hell

One of the vantage points for viewing the Huggins Hell[26] area from above is Myrtle Point.[27] On the morning of August 11, 1925, I walked with a group of men out to the point to see the sunrise. They were members of the third and last Park Commission trip. An hour before sunrise we were up, drinking a quick cup of hot coffee before our walk. We arrived at the point just at daybreak. As the sun came up above the distant horizon, we noticed mist in the valleys below us to the east. As the sun rose higher and the mists of morning lifted from the Porters Flat and Greenbrier area, we stood there awestruck by the whole spectacle and the beauty of a new day beginning.

---

26. Huggins Hell is an exceptionally rugged expanse of Smoky Mountain terrain just below Myrtle Point and bounded by Peregrine Peak, the Boulevard, and Anakeesta Ridge.

27. Myrtle Point is the easternmost of the three peaks of Mount Le Conte. It affords a rocky overlook from which to view the sunrise over the mountains.

From the point we could see the ridges leading off the Boulevard to the south. The ridge between the top of Mount Le Conte and Mount Kephart had an extremely treacherous appearance viewed from any angle. The two main ridges were not only rugged in appearance but were covered with "slicks,"[28] an almost impenetrable mass of Carolina rhododendron, sand myrtle, bush honeysuckle, low-bush blueberry, sawbriers, minnie bush, and many herbaceous plants growing in rock crevices where the soil was thin. Sometimes it was easier to walk on top of these slicks than through them.

Discussion arose about the area known as Huggins Hell. There had been opinions for years as to whether or not Huggins Hell was a volcano cone. No one we knew had gone through it. The wilderness there is very, very rugged. The comment was made that someone ought to explore this area to find out if the two ridges we thought joined each other actually did so. Four or five of us then decided that early in September we would attempt to penetrate Huggins Hell. I was asked to cut a trail from near Myrtle Point to a peak[29] we saw in the distance. We would make our camp there, preparatory to further explorations in this rugged part of the mountains.

My two helpers and I made a trail from just west of Myrtle Point for a distance of about two miles to the peak we had chosen. It took us nearly two days to cut the trail. We returned each night to camp. We had to skirt cliffs and cross the main ridge several times. We found traveling along some sections of the ridge the easiest way and we discovered some spots where low-growing shrubs had been halfbroken, indicating that others had walked this way. Near the peak we cleared out a space on top of the ridge where we could establish a camp.

---

28. In Smoky Mountain parlance, a "slick" refers to a ridgeline or peak covered in impenetrable masses of mountain laurel. From a distance the woody growth appears like a slick place on the ridgeline. When trying to travel through a mountain laurel slick, the mountaineers often referred to it as a "hell."

29. The peak referred to here is Anakeesta Knob, the high point east of Myrtle Point that marks the conjunction of the Boulevard and Anakeesta Ridge. Anakeesta Ridge extends south into Huggins Hell.

CLIFF TOP, MOUNT LE CONTE, AUGUST 22, 1937. ALBERT "DUTCH" ROTH, PHOTOGRAPHER. ALBERT "DUTCH" ROTH DIGITAL PHOTOGRAPH COLLECTION, UNIVERSITY OF TENNESSEE, KNOXVILLE LIBRARIES.

During the second evening, I wrote the others that we had completed the preliminary trail and were ready to go. In early September, we gathered at Mount Le Conte. After supper, we walked to Cliff Top to watch a beautiful sunset. As the sun went down, red in color, the afterglow reflected from low-hanging clouds in the west across the Smoky Mountains many miles away. The colors were so beautiful in the sky that we lingered until dark and needed flashlights to find our way back to the Basin Spring camp.

The five of us—Will Ramsey, Earnest Ogle, F. B. Morgan of the *Knoxville Sentinel*, J. Wylie Brownlee, a Knoxville realtor, and I—were enthusiastic about the upcoming exploratory hike. Smoky Jack would accompany us. Before retiring that night, we packed the supplies and food we judged necessary for three days in the unexplored area. Water, which we would have to carry with us, would be added the following morning from the spring.

Will knew that during the week we would have visitors on the mountain and he knew his dad could help Lavater Whaley take care of them. John Ramsey told us that he had been all around the Huggins Hell area but never into it. He thought this would be a most interesting expedition.

We were up the next morning long before sunup and ate a hearty breakfast. By strong daylight we were on our way. In our trek we crossed Maintop, going down to where the Boulevard and Myrtle Point trails now meet, taking off through the balsam and spruce forest. Smoky Jack led the way, but walking along the improvised trail was very slow.

We arrived at our base camp about 9:30 in the morning. The day was still young, and we decided that we would leave most of our paraphernalia there to lighten our loads as we tried to penetrate the long ridge. I emptied my packsack of everything except bare necessities: a gallon of water in a glass container wrapped in my sheepskin coat, an extra pair of socks, my binoculars, and food. Each of us carried emergency food on our persons and a couple of the fellows had water canteens.

With Will Ramsey in the lead, we made our way slowly down the ridge south to a point where we could determine if these two lower ridges did connect and form a volcanic cone. This was extremely rough traveling. We soon were out of the thin balsam and spruce forest. Rhododendron and the other shrubs which grew abundantly had to be slashed with our bolo knives and machetes so we could get through them. Sometimes it was easier to crawl beneath the heavy growth. We knew that, when we came to the last trees, progress would be even slower. We knew that we would have to walk on top of the tangles of plants to cross the slicks. At times, when we thought we had a good footing, we would drop down three or four feet and sprawl all over the matted, broad-leaved evergreens. After this happened and we had righted ourselves, we would point these places out to the next one following, then he could pick out a better spot to place his foot.

This slick-covered ridge was about a mile long, but it took us nearly two hours to arrive at a point where we could see into the valley far below. We found that the two secondary ridges did not connect. A ravine lay between them.

Our principal mission was over. We decided to eat our lunches and then fight our way back up the main ridge. We would stay there that night and do more exploring the next day. These slicks were always easier to get through going downhill.

On our way down to where we had looked into the valleys, I had been searching likely places for nests of ravens and duck hawks. I had a pair of binoculars. Every so often I would use them to examine the rock ledges and bluffs which appeared to be likely places for these birds to nest. We knew that duck hawks nested near Alum Cave. Were they nesting elsewhere in these mountains? I saw two or three likely places for the nests of large birds. I told my companions that I thought I would cross the valley to the east of us by working down into it along a circuitous route. Then I would pick my way up through an entanglement to the top of another ridge and continue to where I had seen through my binoculars the droppings of some large bird. Earnest and Will offered to go with me, but I thought I could make it all right by myself. I told them I would join them at the base camp that night. It was then just past noon.

I had each of the fellows look through the binoculars at the spot where I hoped to find the nesting site of ravens or duck hawks. I pointed out the way Smoky Jack and I would try to reach that destination. Will observed that, from the looks of those cliffs, I would have to descend a knife ridge. "For goodness sake, be careful," he said.

Smoky Jack and I left the others, who sat on the point and watched us start our descent before they returned to the base camp. It did not take us long to descend the ridge by an indirect route, like sidling downhill. I had a bolo knife in my hands. When I came to a place where I could not drag myself through the underbrush, I used the knife to slash my way. The ascent to the top of another ridge was a little faster than the descent. I found myself near one of the knife ridges. While I worked my way slowly down, Smoky Jack took a rear position. He had been having a difficult time all morning, struggling through the slicks wearing his saddle pockets. I wondered if it might have been better to leave our things at the base camp. Before starting our walk down, I cased my binoculars and placed the case inside my pack. I had very carefully picked out the route to follow and thought I was enough of a woodsman to get where I wanted to go.

I rested a few minutes after arriving at the top of the knife edge. When I was ready to go down the other side, I looked around for Jack. I did not see him, but I guessed he had found something to chase and thought nothing more about it. I knew he could not be too far away.

Going very carefully now and testing each step before putting my whole weight on a rock, I slowly began to descend. One step was wrong. A large slab of rock slipped and plunged into the valley below. I tried to squat, but the weight of my pack pulled me forward and I felt myself sliding. I tried in vain to grab hold of trees and shrubs as I slid past them. My body picked up momentum. I somehow got turned around and found myself going downhill head first, unable to stop. I was knocked unconscious. It must have been an hour and a half or two hours after my fall when consciousness returned. Smoky Jack hovered over me, his tongue stroking my face in rapid licks as he breathed in my face. I slowly opened my eyes. Besides pain in the forehead, my left leg was doubled back under my pack. It hurt me considerably. I lifted one arm to brush the dog's head aside. He barked a short, happy bark and wagged his tail as if to say, "Thank God, you're alive." I raised a hand to my forehead expecting to feel blood, but there was merely swelling. My pack was attached to only one arm strap. I managed to release the other arm and tried to straighten my left leg. It was difficult.

We were in a deep hollow surrounded by the kind of shrubs through which we had fought our way a great part of the morning, as well as some low-growing evergreen trees. I was dazed. It took several minutes to realize that I would live in spite of the pain. I was able to slowly straighten myself out and reach a position with my head uphill instead of down. I looked up to where I had begun sliding and found that I had fallen about two hundred feet. My head must have struck a tree root on the way down because, if it had struck a rock, I am sure I would have been cut or perhaps killed. How the dog found me, I will never know. Perhaps he "air-scented" his way and found me in this manner. I was certain he did not come down the same way I had. He just did not like knife edges.

I tried to rise but fell back to the ground. I thought maybe my leg was broken and, before starting to rise again, felt all around it with my hands. I could not discover any broken bones. I hoped there was nothing wrong with my leg except a bad sprain. I pulled my pack toward me and found that the lower part of it was wet so I emptied it. The binoculars were all right; the loaf of bread was dry and edible; and the chocolate bars were dry. The lower part of my sheepskin coat was wet, and the gallon container of water was broken. This had been wrapped in the coat. I cleaned all the glass out of the pack and repacked it. The dog sat on his haunches watching every move. Once again I tried to get up and this time I was able to stand in spite of my painful knee. I was very thirsty. I had lain there in the hot sun for a long time and my body had dehydrated. I wanted water and I wanted it badly. I tried sucking on the lemon I had with me, but the fruit did not alleviate my thirst. I knew that we had to find water.

I decided to go down into the hollow and find a spring where I could quench my thirst and camp for the night. It was at least three miles back to base camp, too far for me to even try to penetrate such a mass of "slick" country. I would have to whack my way through entanglements all the way up the valley and then onto the top of a ridge. I did not feel equal to it.

Slowly Smoky Jack and I made our way down into the hollow. There was a lot of laurel and rhododendron to cut or crawl through, so the going for the first half-mile was slow. Then we entered the hardwood forest in one of the tributary hollows of Walker Prong. Travel became a little easier here and we could walk faster. I had to "baby" my leg. With each step it hurt a little more. Sometimes Jack followed, sometimes he went ahead of me, looking back over his shoulder every few feet to see if I was following.

One time when he was ahead of me, perhaps halfway between where I had fallen and the spot where we eventually found water, he stopped in his tracks and gave off low, warning growls. He did not come back to me but just stood there. I wondered, "What's wrong with you, why won't you go ahead?" When I reached him, I caught a glimpse of a large bear. The bear took off up the side of the mountain. We went on.

The sun had gone down and we could no longer see its rays on the ridges in back of us when we came to the first water gurgling from the ground. This summer of 1925 was one of the driest the mountains ever had, so I was thankful to find a spring. I took off my pack, lay prone on the ground, and drank. The water was cold and refreshing. The dog chose a spot below me and drank eagerly.

I decided that, instead of trying to walk on downstream, we would camp here. I cleaned the spring out with my bolo knife and made a hollow into which I could dip a cup for easier drinking. Near the spring was a large, fallen log with dried leaves piled against it. I decided I would sleep there. It became cooler, and I knew that I had to collect wood quickly before darkness completely surrounded us. Jack helped drag in firewood. He would find a dead branch and tug at it until he got it moving, then drag it near the woodpile I had started. I cut some green wood with my bolo knife, mostly yellow birch for hot coals that hold heat for a long time. We worked at this job until darkness closed in on us.

As the evening became chillier, I started a small backlog fire about eight feet away from the log against which I intended to sleep. I sat down to contemplate the day's happenings and eat half a loaf of bread and two chocolate bars. I fed Smoky Jack. His pack contained his food for two days, a flashlight, a first-aid kit, a spare set of batteries and bulbs for the light, a couple of pairs of fresh socks for me, fifty feet of grass rope, a drinking cup, matches in a water-tight container, and a piece of rich pine. As soon as I had decided to make camp here, I took my sheepskin coat out of my pack to let the tail of it dry completely before wearing it for the night.

I had no intention of going to sleep early. That would have caused me to awaken too early in the morning. With the dog lying close, ears alert to catch any movement near us, I got to thinking of my companions up on Anakeesta Knob. I knew they would be worried about my safety and would try to find me the next day. Perhaps even now they were talking it over, wondering what had happened to me when I did not show up in camp. I knew approximately where I was, but they did not. If they were to search the next morning, and I was certain they would, they would find the broken water jug and crushed bushes where I had fallen. By these signs they would know that I had gone downstream instead of trying to fight my way back to the base camp. I knew that Will Ramsey was a good tracker and, in all probability, he would figure out that I had gone down the deep ravine to find water.

That night in the deep virgin forest was cold and we needed the fire. I massaged my knee frequently and tried to give it a little exercise so it would not stiffen. About two and a half hours after complete darkness, I replenished the fire, put on my coat, and lay down alongside the log. Smoky Jack came over and took his sleeping position against my legs. Before going to sleep I prayed, thanking God that I had not been seriously hurt and asking Him to let me return to the Basin Spring camp the following day. Two or three times during the night, when my legs began to get cold, I replenished the fire. Once I went to the spring and drank. The dog got up and stretched with me. When I lay down again, he snuggled up against me.

The sun was rising when I awakened the next day. I was stiff, but I took a few exercises putting my left, "game" leg through more than I did the right. I drank some water, ate some bread and two more chocolate bars, and fed Jack. I extinguished the fire, strapped on Jack's saddle pockets, shouldered my own packsack, and limped down through the woods.

Highbush blueberries were ripe. There were a few of the intermediate species, too, and each time I would come to one of them I would grab a handful and eat them. I found several edible mushrooms but they need cooking to make them palatable, so I paid no attention to them.

I knew that sooner or later we would arrive at the Alum Cave Trail or, at least, Alum Cave Creek. I was familiar with that creek because I had fished the stream many times for speckled trout. Now and then I had to cut through rhododendron. I tried to go around these thickets when I could. In one doghobble-infested area, I found the nest of a black-throated blue warbler with young in it. The parent birds did not take kindly to our intrusion and tried to drive us away.

About a hundred yards below the nest, I came to familiar territory, the stream where I had fished many times. Now I knew where the trail was. I decided to go back to the top of Mount Le Conte instead of to the Grassy Patch Cabin[30] and from there walk on down to Dave Ogle's store.

I had not gone far when I heard voices above me. Someone was coming my way. I sat down in the trail to wait. In about ten minutes, a group of Boy Scouts who had hiked to the top of Mount Le Conte the preceding day reached me. Wylie Brownlee had gone back to the Basin Spring camp to report my absence. The boys' scoutmaster sent them down this trail, telling them not to leave it, and to go as far as the Grassy Patch Cabin. He sent food for me by them. Smoky Jack and I were within half a mile of Alum Cave when they saw us. They told me they had been hungry and had eaten all the food at the cave before coming on down the trail. That did me little good! I was very hungry and some solid food in my stomach would have helped me.

We met a little past noon. I asked the boys to return to camp and tell those there to quit looking for me since I was on my way up. But I knew that it would be a long, hard climb. They should have made the climb in less than two hours, but I found out later that they dilly-dallied along the way and the sun was just about to set before they arrived back in camp to report that they had found me unharmed.

I rested more often going up the trail than I had ever rested before or since. My knee hurt me. Every time it hurt too badly, I would sit down in the trail or on a rock and rest. Nearly every time I did this, Smoky Jack would come over and sit on his haunches or lay his head across my knees. I would rest about five minutes and then walk on again. During these rests I would massage my knee, which helped the pain. I picked up a stick to help with uphill climbing.

I was afraid that I might have trouble getting around the rockslide above Alum Cave, but I found plenty of shrubs to grasp. I dragged myself without once slipping. We had two miles to walk after reaching the ridge on top of Alum Cave and the going was slow. The sun was just

---

30. Originally a possession cabin built for the Champion Fibre Company, the Grassy Patch Cabin stood at the confluence of Alum Cave Creek and Walker Prong. The site is now occupied by the parking area at the head of the Alum Cave Trail.

about to set when we arrived within a quarter of a mile of the present campground. While we rested, I called the dog over to me and took out the flashlight in his pack. I thought I might need it.

I had just started up the trail once more when I heard from above two familiar voices. Instead of stopping to wait for them, we climbed on. Even the dog recognized the voices of Will Ramsey and Earnest Ogle and ran ahead of me, wagging his tail. As they saw me, we yelled to each other and they hurried down to me. They got on either side of me and placed their arms under my shoulders to help me. I laughed, "Fellows, I don't need this sort of assistance so near home base."

Will had found my broken water bottle that morning and discovered where I had slashed underbrush. He saw footprints in soft earth beneath rhododendrons and realized I had gone down the ravine. He returned to base camp while three men retraced their steps to the camp on top of Mount Le Conte.

Wylie Brownlee and F. B. Morgan had gone into Gatlinburg, and then to Knoxville, to organize search parties to comb the mountains. They had helped pack the provisions remaining at base camp and had left the top of the mountain before the Boy Scouts had scarcely returned to camp with their report.

John Ramsey thought I should have a good alcohol rubdown on my left leg. All took turns doing that. I slept well that night and awoke the next morning feeling as fresh as ever.

Someone had to go down the mountain and announce that the lost had been found. Will and John Ramsey, Smoky Jack, and I made the hike down without too much difficulty, got into my car at Cherokee Orchard, and drove into Gatlinburg. There we found men gathering for a search. Others would come in later from Knoxville, we were told. I called Colonel Chapman from the Mountain View Hotel. He was glad to hear my voice. He told me the Knoxville newspapers had already printed news about my being lost, perhaps killed, or wandering around in unknown territory, and that a lot of my Smoky Mountains Hiking Club friends were concerned about me and ready to help in the search. The colonel told me he would tell the newspapers that I had walked out by myself. He thought it would be best if I made my appearance soon in Knoxville.

MEMBERS OF THE ROTARY CLUB ON MOUNT LE CONTE. ALBERT "DUTCH" ROTH ON FAR LEFT, PAUL ADAMS AND SMOKY JACK WITH SADDLE POCKETS ON FAR RIGHT, JIM THOMPSON, PHOTOGRAPHER, SECOND FROM RIGHT. THOMPSON BROTHERS DIGITAL PHOTOGRAPH COLLECTION, UNIVERSITY OF TENNESSEE, KNOXVILLE LIBRARIES.

Will Ramsey, Smoky Jack, and I drove on into Knoxville, arriving shortly after the afternoon newspapers had hit the streets. The colonel was not successful in stopping headline news, but the later editions and the *Knoxville Journal* the following morning printed updated stories. The Associated Press and United Press International had picked up the story, sending it out over their wire services.

My mother and sister, who were in Toledo, Ohio, heard nothing of the episode. My brother, Bob, who was working in Detroit, called them to tell them I had been found. My father, who was returning to Knoxville from Arkansas, bought a paper in Memphis and read the account of my being lost. When he arrived in Nashville, he had to hurry to the Tennessee Central Railroad to make connections with a Knoxville-bound train and was unable to buy a later edition of a Nashville paper. The conductor on the train told him the missing son had been found and was perfectly all right.

Father later confessed to me that he had given some thought to my funeral arrangements. My sister, Jean, has always believed that Smoky Jack saved my life. She may have been right.

CHAPTER ELEVEN

Accident at Last Water

On October 10, 1925, we had snow on top of Mount Le Conte. The first snowfall was only four inches deep and melted away in five days. We were to have many more storms, some lasting for more than two days with accumulations of more than five feet. We were to be marooned later in the winter because of the snow's depth.

I wanted to spend Christmas and New Year's with my family in Knoxville, but in November some University of Tennessee students asked for a hunting trip over those holidays. So I spent the holidays on top of the mountain.

On Christmas Eve, the crowd of university students hiked up the mountain to hunt. But the snow was so deep and the weather so cold—several degrees below zero most of their stay—there was no hunting. One of the young fellows drank from a bottle too often on his way up and came into camp with frozen hands and feet. It took three or four of his companions to hold him while the rest of us tried to bring back

circulation into those parts of his body by keeping them in cold water
and not letting him get too close to the hot stove. We were able to thaw
him out in about two hours with no apparent after effects. This group
stayed close to the fire, refusing even to go to Cliff Top to view sunsets,
although I kept that trail open. The students returned to Knoxville on
December 27th. Smoky Jack and I came down the mountain with them.

Jim Thompson,[31] a leading outdoor photographer in Knoxville, told
me that sometimes Rainbow Falls freezes, or so he had heard. I had been

---

31. James Edward "Jim" Thompson (1880–1976), a noted Knoxville professional photographer,
was among the charter members of the Great Smoky Mountains Hiking Club. Thompson
and his brother Robin photographed the Smokies extensively in the 1920s. Jim Thompson's
images were used by Colonel David Chapman to promote the Great Smoky Mountains to a
congressional committee as a potential site for a national park.

told the same thing. Jim said he wished to make pictures of it, if it froze, and I told him that I would try to keep him informed.

Jack and I later explored Rainbow Falls. We found a high ice cone at its base in sort of a stalagmite formation about twenty-five feet high. There was also a very large, more or less irregular icicle hanging from the top of the falls. This was what Jim Thompson wanted to photograph. I drove into Knoxville to spend the night at home and called Jim to tell him that Rainbow Falls was frozen. We agreed to meet on December 29th at Cherokee Orchard and start the climb with his cameras, tripods, and other paraphernalia needed for good pictures of the frozen spectacle.

On the appointed day, Smoky Jack and I stopped first at Ogle's store for supplies, food for me, and twenty pounds of shingle nails for the dog to carry. I packed our supplies and waited for Jim and his crew. They showed up soon, drove ahead of us to the Orchard, and started up the mountain without waiting for our slower car. We drove near the old barn, where we parked, and I saw the tail end of Jim's party. I called to them and said I would be along shortly. Smoky Jack with his saddle pockets and I with my pack started up the trail. We caught up with the men before they reached the end of the horseback trail.

We arrived at the falls about ten o'clock. The formations at the top and bottom of the falls were much larger than when Jack and I had found them a couple of days earlier. I knew we would be here for some time. While Jim took pictures from every angle, I built a fire so we could warm ourselves and eat our lunches.

It was too bad that we did not have color film for photography on that trip. There was a sort of iridescent aqua blue in the ice where bright sunlight struck both the great ice hunk at the bottom and the large icicle protruding from the top. It was a truly magnificent sight. Jim had the cameras set up at various locations to take pictures of this phenomenon. We all took turns getting into the pictures, even Smoky Jack.

I had no idea how long Jim and his crew planned to stay. By mid-afternoon, I told them that Jack and I had better be going on up the mountain if we expected to get into camp before dark. We bid each other goodbye. I strapped on Smoky Jack's saddle pockets and shouldered my pack. I asked the fellows to please put the fire out before they left. After

FROZEN RAINBOW FALLS, DECEMBER 1925. JIM THOMPSON, PHOTOGRAPHER.
THOMPSON BROTHERS DIGITAL PHOTOGRAPH COLLECTION, UNIVERSITY OF
TENNESSEE, KNOXVILLE LIBRARIES.

gaining the top of the falls, I walked over and called to them. They had
started packing up their cameras for the return trip. Jack and I walked on
up the mountain. We had not gone far when I found that the tracks we
had made a few days earlier were now covered with about three inches
of fresh snow. This caused us some difficulties. We rested often since

both of us were heavily laden. Beyond Twin Falls I realized by the setting sun that we were not going to walk into camp before dark. We did not rest again until we had reached Last Water. It had been getting steadily colder by degrees during our climb and both of us were slipping and sliding as we worked our way upward.

At the last crossing of Le Conte Creek, while I sat and rested, I took a five-celled flashlight out of my pack. It was cold to the touch. The temperature must have been zero. We had already entered the spruce fir forest. I wore long johns, wool britches, two pairs of wool socks, a heavy wool shirt, a jacket, and a sheepskin coat on the outside. My head was covered with a heavy cap with ear and neck flaps, the lower part of which could be tied at the throat. On my hands, I wore a pair of fleece-lined bearskin gloves with cuffs nearly reaching my elbows. In spite of all that clothing, if I rested more than a few minutes I became chilled.

We got a drink of water, then I reshouldered my pack. We crossed the creek and started on up the mountain. We were now in complete darkness. Smoky Jack was already past the clay bank which was covered with ice. I was halfway across this treacherous place when it happened. I fell on the ice cake. The flashlight was damaged in my fall. I fumbled around and unscrewed the end of the light to find it empty of extra bulbs. I knew right then we were in trouble. Somehow, I managed to crawl above the ice cake and reach a level part of the trail.

What to do was a question flashing through my mind. We had more than a mile to go. I had only a few matches with me, certainly not enough to light my way on up the mountain. I did have a piece of rich pine and a short candle, but these probably would not outlast the emergency. Should we pace part of the trail all night long or until daylight to keep from freezing to death? Should I attempt to build a fire of wet wood and hover over it for the rest of the night?

Smoky Jack had on his collar without a lead chain, so I decided to improvise a chain. Perhaps he could lead me into camp. He could see in the dark. I was the one who could not, certainly not in this dark forest. I took off Jack's saddle pockets and got a handful of nails. Then I unfastened my coat and jacket, took the belt out of my britches and pleated the pants at the hips, forcing nails through the cloth to secure them to my body. I refastened my short jacket and took the belt out of my sheepskin coat. Before pleating and fastening the outer coat as close to myself as possible, I reached into my pack and took out all the articles—including fresh eggs—I knew intense freezing would hurt and put them into the coat's inner lining.

I spliced the two belts together with nails. Reaching under Jack's collar, I nailed one end of my improvised lead rope to it, keeping a hold on the other end. I lit a match or two to find a broken tree limb where I could hang my pack six or seven feet above the ground. I placed the dog's saddle pockets near the base of the tree and told him to lead me up the trail. He must have realized my predicament because he did not take any of his usual shortcuts that night as he slowly led the way. He sensed that I could not see in the darkness. I stumbled and fell several times in our upward climb but, luckily, did not break any bones. The dog did not want to hurry and he did not strain against the leash as he would have if he had been tracking. When I fell he would stop, turn around, and wait for me to get up. At the switchbacks where the trail changed directions, he would give a little jerk or two on the leash to let me know that there was a change of direction. When I turned to take that direction, he would let me know that I was following the proper trail by giving off a low, reassuring bark. I was not cold. I was exercising too hard to be cold.

After an hour and a half of walking in complete darkness, we reached the clearing. I could discern a little light reflected from a clear sky sprinkled with stars. In another five minutes we were in the cabin. I lit a kerosene lantern, touched a match to the fire which had been laid before we left the cabin, and unfastened the improvised leash from Jack's collar to give him full liberty. I waited until the cabin warmed up a bit before removing my outer coat and jacket.

After warming myself, I unpacked the few provisions I had taken from my packsack. I found that two of the twenty-four eggs I had tried to get up the mountain were broken. Why the others were not broken is a mystery I will never understand. But the eggs were all frozen! A few pieces of beefsteak were frozen solidly. A few apples also had frozen, as well as the fresh oranges and bananas, but they would still be palatable if eaten soon.

I went to the spring to get two buckets of water. As I left the cabin, I raised my lantern high to see the thermometer hanging in a tree just a few feet away. It registered twenty-five degrees below zero. During the two-hundred-foot walk from the spring, ice had formed on the surface of the water in the buckets.

I was hungry. I had steak, boiled potatoes, canned spinach, coleslaw, and my regular amount of hot chocolate made with powdered milk. I fed Jack an extra ration of dog biscuits and let him lie on the floor and chew on the bone from the steak. I gave him a little gravy, too. I reached down to pet him occasionally and talked to him, telling him what a good job he had done in leading me through the dark forest to the safety of our cabin. Sometimes he would thump his tail against the puncheon floor of the cabin. He would watch me out of the corners of his eyes as I moved about or sat and read.

Around our normal bedtime Jack got up, stretched, and then wanted out. I tried to get him to stay inside with me, but he still wanted out. I watched him enter his kennel. He turned around a time or two and scratched balsam needles into a hollow where he curled up to sleep. I kept the fire in the stove burning all night, arising from between my blankets every three hours or so to replenish the wood.

The outside temperature the next morning was thirty-two degrees below zero. After a leisurely breakfast, Jack and I walked down the mountain to retrieve our packs. I saw many places where I had fallen, what I had tripped over, where the dog had been careful when he made a turn on the switchback trail, and where he had kept to that trail the night before and not taken any of his usual cutoffs. We were back at our cabin within two hours.

The next day brought a few fellows who wanted to celebrate New Year's Eve on Mount Le Conte. They came for one night only, saying that it was too cold up there to suit them and that they could not understand why I wanted to stay there all winter long. The temperature dropped to thirty-seven degrees below zero for the second time that winter. Smoky Jack and I did not accompany this group down the mountain.

Snow started falling late that evening and was still falling when we arose the next morning. I had to shovel a new path out to the spring when the snow stopped. Now there was a depth of two and a half feet of snow on the mountaintop.

We were snowed in, sure enough, but warm and happy!

CHAPTER TWELVE

A Nose for Tracking

In the course of learning about the environs of Mount Le Conte in the Great Smoky Mountains, I met many of the native families who lived at the foot of this isolated peak. This was true of the other mountains in the range, particularly on the Tennessee side. I knew very few people on the North Carolina side, but one was Horace Kephart[32] of writing fame. I had been with him in the forests where we studied birds and hunted and fished.

I knew one or two families who lived part of the year in North Carolina on top of the range's vast balds and another part of the year in

---

32. Horace Kephart (1862–1931), author and outdoorsman, is best known for *Our Southern High-landers*, a chronicle of manners and customs of the Smoky mountaineers at the beginning of the twentieth century. Kephart's writings were influential in promoting the establishment of the Great Smoky Mountains National Park.

Tennessee. I will not say too much of their "trades" or the reasons they lived in both states, but it is a well-known fact that the Hall Cabin[33] near Silers Bald[34] was built purposely on the state line, half of it being in North Carolina and half in Tennessee. I have heard that state revenuers, hunting for stills, slept on one side of the cabin, in one state, and their quarry stayed in the other half of the cabin, not daring to cross to the opposite side for fear of being arrested. The residents continued to live this way until the revenuers departed.

When I started the conservation camp on top of Mount Le Conte, which later developed into LeConte Lodge, I worked closely with Lewis McCarter,[35] a ranger for the Champion Fibre Company, owner of Mount Le Conte and vast acres of land behind Greenbrier toward Mount Guyot. At the time I operated the camp, McCarter was considered one of the best guides in the Gatlinburg area. He visited me on top of the mountain about once a month. Because he was constantly on trails and old roads in this untouched timberland, we agreed that I would take care of some of his duties on the upper reaches of the mountain, thus relieving him of part of his patrol work.

When he visited the top of the mountain, McCarter could not arrive unannounced. Smoky Jack would always answer his dogs' barking as they approached the camp. Then I would usually chain my dog. It would not have been right if Jack had hurt one of Lewis's dogs.

One day in early fall, Lewis suggested that the two of us, two of his sons, and his dogs take a week off from our duties and go to the Hall Cabin on Silers Bald, packing our supplies on horses. I questioned the possibility of getting horses to Silers Bald across Clingmans Dome, but

33. Adams mistakenly identifies Hall Cabin as being on Silers Bald. The Hall Cabin was located on Derrick Knob on the main Smoky divide six miles west of Silers Bald. By the time Adams was staying on Mount Le Conte, the Hall Cabin had burned down.

34. Silers Bald, a high peak on the main Smoky divide about four miles west of Clingmans Dome, is one of the well-known grassy balds of the western end of the Smokies.

35. Louis or Lewis McCarter (1879–1960) is identified in the 1920, 1930, and 1940 United States Census as a Gatlinburg farmer, lumberman, and "patrolman." During the 1920s, he was employed as a field agent for the Champion Fibre Company.

he assured me he had done it. We decided to wait until the crowds at camp would not be so large. I could leave Smoky Jack with my two helpers for several days.

Smoky Jack had been with me down the Alum Cave Trail to the Grassy Patch Cabin, a forester's cabin at the junction of Alum Cave Creek and the Walker Prong of the Little Pigeon River, and from there on down through the Sugarlands area and into Gatlinburg. But he had never been upriver on the old Indian Gap Road.

When I left camp early on the appointed morning, I cautioned my helpers to keep Smoky Jack chained most of the time. I was afraid he might take a notion to follow me. I petted the dog and tried to explain that he should take orders from Earnest and Lavater. He liked both of them.

I was to meet Lewis McCarter at the junction of Alum Cave Trail and Indian Gap Trail at six o'clock. We would try to reach our destination in one day. The sky was clear, the weather warm. It did not take me long—perhaps two hours to make the descent of nearly six miles. I arrived at our meeting place a few minutes before I heard Lewis, his boys, the dogs, and the packhorses coming up the old road. He gave his horses a short time to rest before we started on toward Indian Gap. It was just long enough to tie my sheathed rifle, a couple of army blankets, and a few personal items to one of the packs. We made our way up Indian Gap Trail. At the last ford of the Indian Gap prong of the river, we let the horses drink their fill. It would be many miles before we could again water them. In the gap, we let the horses rest and graze for a few minutes before pushing on toward Mount Collins and then to the top of Clingmans Dome.

About noon, we topped heavily forested Clingmans Dome and yet the most difficult part of the trail was yet to come. I did not know how we were going to get those pack horses along or around the state-line ridge. In a few places it is just wide enough for a trail. Sometimes it is dangerous for a man to walk along, let alone a packed horse. But Lewis and his boys did not always keep their horses on top of the ridge. They led them off the trail, either on the North Carolina side of the ridge or on the Tennessee side of the mountain, slowly picking out the easiest way for the horses. The four of us walked all the way, with the two boys leading the horses and Lewis pointing out the best way to reach the far side of a "hog-back" along the state line. Until that particular day, I did not think horses could get around some of those rough, mountainous areas. But the McCarters were sure of themselves. They proved to me that it could be done without being too dangerous. We made so much racket traveling through the forest that we saw very little game—it could hear us coming and make itself scarce before we got within shooting distance. Before nightfall, we came to the Hall Cabin. We had come to hunt squirrels, grouse, and turkeys and to fish the upper Forney and Hazel Creeks, plus enjoy ourselves in primitive forests. And so we did.

We pitched in and cleaned up the cabin—at least, clean enough for us to live in for the few days we would be there. We unpacked the horses, tethered, and watered them. One of the boys went to the spring for cooking and washing water and we ate our first meal in the cabin. The horses had had a hard day, but Lewis was taking no chances. Most of the time he tethered them on the grassy bald.

We hunted and fished for four days. At every meal with the exception of the night we arrived, our dining table held some sort of game or fish. During the third afternoon, Lewis and I were trout fishing in the headwaters of Hazel Creek when the sky started to cloud over. Before we could get back to the cabin, rain came down in torrents. The rain was so heavy that we both were soaked to the skin. Lewis's boys had a good fire going in the fireplace and had prepared grouse and gray squirrels for supper. We decided to save our fish for breakfast the next morning. Rain fell in torrents most of that night, but the sky cleared by morning.

The following evening, we watched the sunset from the bald. I was using my binoculars to determine which species of ground birds were feeding among the grasses. As I scanned the area, one of Lewis's boys said he saw a wolf, the same one we had seen on Mount Le Conte, coming in a slow trot from a spot a half-mile to our east. I turned my binoculars in that direction. Imagine my surprise when I saw, instead of a wolf, Smoky Jack! His nose was to the ground and whiffing the air, too. He did not have on his collar so there was no "tell-tale" sign of any rope or chain. When he reached a spot where he smelled fresh scents—I had stood for several minutes that day in that spot, he became quite excited. With leaps and bounds he came straight for us. I started to stand, but Lewis asked me to stay where I was and see which of us Jack would come to first. We were sitting about six or eight feet apart, but there was no doubt in my mind who he would choose.

Smoky Jack came directly to me and seemed surprised and elated to find me. He leaped about, half-howling and half-crying with joy. After perhaps a minute of this display, he quieted and lay down close to me. I petted and talked to him, wondering if he had slipped his collar because it had not been buckled tightly enough or if he had swelled his neck when the boys back on Mount Le Conte put the collar on him, thus outsmarting them.

Lewis's pack of mongrels and Smoky Jack got along fine together during the remaining two days we were on the mountain. He left them alone and they left him alone. He usually stayed by my side. We did not invite trouble by feeding the dogs together.

We wondered how Jack picked up our trail five days old and followed us. To my knowledge he had never been up the old Indian Gap Road or across Mount Collins and Clingmans Dome. When Smoky Jack and I returned to the top of Mount Le Conte, the boys told me the story of how Jack had started out to find me.

On the second day after I left, one of the boys took Smoky Jack with him when he hiked down to Gatlinburg to pick up supplies. They made the hike in normal time and the dog was fed as soon as they arrived back in camp. Then he was chained until the next day when the boys would be working around camp and could keep their eyes on him.

Then the rain came to the top of Mount Le Conte the same as it did on Silers Bald. About the middle of the next morning, one of the boys took the dog's collar off and they walked to the spring together to get fresh water. They recollared him when they returned from the spring, and, with their breakfast over, they walked to the east of Basin Spring to work. When they came back to camp to prepare their noon meal, the dog was gone! He had managed to slip his collar. They tracked him on the wet ground to the start of the Alum Cave Trail and then returned to camp.

They did not worry too much about Jack. They thought perhaps if he did not find me he would go down to Earnest's home. He had been there many times before to wait until someone came for him. Or perhaps he would return to the top of the mountain.

I walked over to examine Jack's collar. The boys told me that they had not bothered it at all, just let it lie there. The stem of the buckle was in the first hole of the collar. Normally, it should have been in the third hole.

I knew Jack had swelled his neck.

CHAPTER THIRTEEN

Work for Ramsey and Huff

S nows fell, one on top of the other, during the winter of 1925-26. Much of the time the snow was too deep for us to go down the mountain. Although marooned, Jack and I were happy. Each time I went to the spring or walked to Cliff Top, Jack was with me. He seemed content as he ran through the woods. Watching him struggle in deep snow was fascinating. He would lunge into the deep stuff like a charging bull, get stuck, turn around, run back a few feet, brace himself, and make another lunge. He repeated this comical routine time and time again.

I kept myself busy by splitting out shingles for the cabin, cutting firewood, keeping the trail to the spring clear for easy walking, and keeping a trail open to Cliff Top. I liked to hike out there once a day, usually late in the afternoon, so I could see the snow-clad spectacle.

We ate well. Since I had wanted to spend the winter in the camp, I had brought in a good supply of canned and dried foods and other supplies late in the fall of 1925. I also killed some small wild game at various times for the supper meal.

In early February, the gigantic icicle and the ice stalagmite at Rainbow Falls had disappeared. There was no snow below the Orchard. There was no vegetation springing into growth, except a couple of hepatica plants were in bloom. This was a welcome flower for it has always been a sign of spring to me. I still look for it each year near winter's end.

After our early February hike, Jack and I were not able to make another trip until the latter part of March. Snows continued to pile up. We had plenty of stove wood and we did not suffer from lack of food or shelter, so we were comfortable. The temperatures during most of February and March were not as intensely cold as they had been around the first of the year. When weather permitted, I added new cooking and eating tables, built a few cooking fireplaces, and prepared for 1926's busy season.

We were always too busy on top of the mountain to be lonesome. When I felt the need to communicate with human beings, I would sit down at my typewriter and write letters. The epistles served as a tonic for my mind.

Smoky Jack usually spent the evenings inside the cabin with me. He would lie quietly curled up, with one ear always erect to catch any strange sound. Whenever the long-tailed deer mice became playful in the cabin walls, he would go over to the spot and run his long nose along the wall near them. They would scurry away. If the mice were moving in the upper part of the cabin, the dog would jump up onto one of the bunks and examine that part of the wall. He did not like to hear them prowling around disturbing the quiet of the cabin, its stillness broken only by the crackling of burning wood.

When Jack had to walk through water in the winter, retained water would later freeze between his toes. Ice between an animal's toes can be very painful.

At such times Jack would come limping to me, lie down at my feet, and roll over on his back, sticking all four feet in the air. Sometimes he would whine a little and I always knew what was wrong. I would remove my gloves and with my fingers pick out the ice, then massage his feet.

He would afterward stand and bark, as if thanking me. These occasions were rare. I tried to keep him out of the water.

After hiking down the mountain a few times with Smoky Jack, I decided that the accumulated snow had melted enough to send him to the store alone. I put his saddle pockets on him one morning and, leading him to the perimeter of the camp yard, I said, "Jack, go to the store." He went obediently. It had been a full three months since he had been down and back by himself, but he made the trip in the normal time.

By the end of March, I was almost ready for the crowds of hikers. They came only on weekends at first, but we were busier as April arrived and the season advanced.

I thought it best to have Lavater Whaley return as a regular employee. I had talked it over with him, but he wanted to wait until the first of May before starting. Earnest Ogle was not available to work with me. He had married and was not willing in his early months of marriage to work on the mountain. He recommended a young man named Maples. I discussed this matter with Lavater. He said they had gone to school together and he could get along fine with the fellow. It was decided that they would come to the top of the mountain around May 1st for the summer's work.

Meantime, I had gone into Knoxville a time or two. Each time I went I talked to Colonel Chapman, who always seemed pleased to get my report on camp activities. I saw a few other members of the Conservation Association. I gave them accounts of what I had done all winter on the mountain—how we were ready for new crowds, of the new tables and fireplaces I had built, and how I had improved some of the trails. I also attended one board meeting of the Association, at which I gave a full report of the camp's progress. I was asked many questions. I thought things were running smoothly and returned to the top of the mountain that same day.

A few days later, I sent Smoky Jack to the store. While unpacking his saddle pockets after his return, I noticed an enclosed letter from Colonel Chapman.

After reading the letter, I cried. It was a letter of dismissal, effective as of May 10th. The colonel had been kind in his selection of words and told me how he had fought a one-sided battle for me to remain there until the coming season was over. But he was only one of five camp committeemen and four of them thought it was best that I be dismissed. Jack Huff[36] was to be appointed to the job. His helpers would be Will Ramsey and other mountain men, some of whom I did not know. It was very disheartening to me. I had worked so hard in the interests of the Association and had looked forward to this 1926 season.

Now what was I to do?

What was I to do with Smoky Jack?

I went into Knoxville and talked to three of the five committeemen in attempts to change their minds and let me stay, but to no avail. The secretaries of the two other members informed me that the men I wanted to see were out of town. I saw one of these two on the street that day and called to him. When he saw me, he walked away swiftly and disappeared into a department store.

I talked to Colonel Chapman. There were tears in his eyes as we conversed.

I told him I did not have any firm plans, but I had considered setting myself up as a nature study guide in Gatlinburg, taking parties into the mountains. He thought this might be a more profitable occupation than the position I had held for the Association and would bring me more income. He promised to send me customers. I had no hard feelings against the colonel and the other committeemen. (I am now sure in my own mind that the Conservation Association members regretted two months later that they had not retained me.)

I told the Colonel that I could operate the camp until May 10th or quit now, if he thought it best. He did not. He said he never liked a quitter and he knew that my knowledge of nature study would stand me in good stead. The hard part of my situation was that I had to go to Lavater and the Maples boy and tell them of the changed circumstances. If they

---

36. Estel Carl Huff (1903–1985), affectionately called "Jack" by those who knew him, is identified in the 1930 United States Census as a forest ranger for the "Smoky Mt. Park." Jack Huff is the son of Andy Huff, the proprietor of the Mountain View Hotel.

wanted to retain their jobs at the camp, they would have to talk to Jack Huff and Will Ramsey. Lavater told me he would look for other work and the Maples boy did not seem too enthusiastic to continue work.

Back in Gatlinburg, I stopped at the hotel to discuss my new work plans with Andy Huff, Jack's father. He thought something might be worked out to use me as a guide, but he asked that I give him a little time to think about it. He had been using Will Ramsey as one of his two guides for hotel patrons, so he probably realized he would need to hire another guide.

Smoky Jack and I were back in Gatlinburg the following week and met Will Ramsey on the main street. We spoke as we passed. We were a little way apart when he called to me, asking if I had any hard feelings toward him. I told him, "No." He then asked what I was going to do after May 10th. I told him about my little talk with Andy. He assured me that he would put in a good word for me because this season he would not be in a position to do guide work for the hotel.

Both Ramsey and Huff visited the camp a couple of times before their takeover. They wanted to go over the inventory, particularly of the tools. They planned to build a much larger cabin with a fireplace. We met on friendly terms and there was no animosity from any of us. Will told me he had talked to Andy, who wanted to see me at my earliest convenience. Jack Huff thought that arrangements might be worked out between us so that I could do guide work for the hotel.

But what was I to do with Smoky Jack? Should I sell him or take him into Knoxville to my parents and sister? My sister, Jean, wanted him to live at our home. I wanted to keep him in the mountains, if possible, for I knew that he would be happier where he could still pack up the mountain occasionally when I guided hiking parties.

The week before I left my employment on top of Mount Le Conte, Andy Huff told me I could erect a tent on a platform near a small walled-up spring in the southwest corner of the hotel yard to live in during the guiding season. He said I could take my meals at the hotel with the family. But he did not want me to keep the dog on the premises. He had his reasons for this, of course, and I did not question them. So I told Jean that if she thought she could manage Jack, I would bring him to Knoxville.

The morning of May 10th rolled around and Jack Huff, Will Ramsey, and four or five men, only one of whom I knew, arrived to take over the camp. The transfer was smooth. I showed Will and Jack my record books and turned over what camp money I had. They persuaded me to stay and have dinner. I was asked during the meal what I was going to do with Smoky Jack and I told them I was taking him to my Knoxville home the next day.

Will asked, "Paul, why don't you leave the dog here with us, to be worked? We will treat him kindly."

I said, "Will, I don't think the dog will work for you fellows. He has been with me over a year, and we have become very close; I just don't think he'll work for you as he has for me. I know that you think a lot of him, and he thinks a lot of you, but I don't think he will stay on the mountain unchained as he has been most of the time. He will pick up my trail and follow me."

We talked for some time about the situation. After turning the matter over in my mind, I decided to leave Jack.

I was by myself as I walked down the mountain that afternoon, climbed into my car at the Orchard, and drove toward Gatlinburg. Will had had to chain Jack when I left. The dog probably realized a change was taking place. He had been very attentive to me all morning. It was with deep regret that I left him at the camp. I had Will and Jack's promise that the dog would never be packed with more than thirty pounds for his trips up the mountain. I knew he would not be as long as Will was there. I had to believe that the dog would not be abused.

I spent the night at the hotel. The next morning, I erected my tent on the platform, moved a cot into it, and borrowed a small table from Mrs. Huff. She also supplied a couple of chairs for my new quarters. I walked up to Ogle's store and bought a kerosene lamp, as well as bedding.

Charlie Ogle was surprised to see that Smoky Jack was not with me. When he found out that I had left the dog on the mountaintop to work for Will and Jack, he told me that it would not work out at all. He thought the dog would slip off and come to me. He also said that, if I did not want the dog to live in Knoxville, there were several families right around Gatlinburg who would be glad to keep him for me. He offered to keep him, but I told Charlie that we were going to give this new venture a try. If it did not work out satisfactorily, I would bring Jack off the mountain and make other arrangements.

That night I was aroused from my sleep in the tent when Smoky Jack laid his head across my chest. He was breathing hard and was collarless. I ran a hand out from under the covers and patted the dog's head. He lay on the planked tent floor beside me the rest of the night.

Early the next morning, Will Ramsey arrived with Jack's collar and chain.

He had chained Jack the night before, but Jack had broken loose to search for me. He led Smoky Jack away from me toward the store, where he had left the saddle pockets and his own packsack. The dog looked back over his shoulder at me several times. His eyes were accusing.

There was no guiding trip to make that day. I drove in to Knoxville where I hoped to drum up trade. My first stop was Colonel Chapman's office. I told him the transfer had gone off smoothly and that I was in Knoxville that day to make contacts for guiding hikers. He assured me that within two or three weeks I would be kept busy. From his office I drove to the University of Tennessee to the zoological and botany departments. There I explained to the heads of the departments what I was going to do this summer. They thought it was a good idea. I then drove to the Chamber of Commerce, the Knoxville Tourist Bureau, and the Knoxville Automobile Club, explaining the situation to all of them.

Later I drove out to see Mother and Jean. They were very disappointed that I had not brought Smoky Jack to them. Mother told me, "Paul, you know as well as I do that Smoky Jack will look you up every time he can break loose or get close to the store. He loves you and it will not work out. You'll have to bring him to us later on."

I drove back to Gatlinburg late that evening after eating supper with my family. Father was home for a few days between pastoral duties, so he and I had a long talk together on the front porch. He thought that my idea of doing nature study guide work was a labor I would enjoy. He wished me every success in the venture.

After the first of June, I was kept very busy for the remainder of the tourist season. One morning that month, I guided a party over to Norton Creek to view the extremely large yellow poplars which grew there. The owner of the property liked to see large trees growing and would not permit those trees to be cut for lumber. Anyone wanting to see them was welcome to visit the area any time. The hike down the river to the mouth of Norton Creek was a beautiful walk of about a mile and a half below the hotel. The road over which we walked followed the east side of the river and crossed it on a rickety old bridge.

Two gigantic poplar trees stood close together. They were eight and nine feet in diameter. The lowest limbs were at least eighty feet above the ground. We were standing there beside the trees when we heard the barking of dogs in the farmyard.

To my surprise, I saw Smoky Jack with his saddle pockets on, coming directly to me. He leaped across the high pasture fence and came on into the woods. One of the party suggested that we start back for the hotel at once so that Jack could be returned to the top of the mountain. I

said, "No, we'll finish this hike. Whoever brought him off the mountain doesn't know where to look for him. I know that he slipped away and followed us down here. We will keep him with us."

After eating lunch on the ridge above Norton Creek, we returned at a leisurely pace to the hotel. I identified plants and rocks and birds and answered many questions. I shared my lunch with Smoky Jack. By the middle of the afternoon, we were back at the hotel and I chained Jack to one of the posts holding up the tent platform. I fed him then turned him loose for a little while before rechaining him to the post.

The next morning it was not Will Ramsey who came for the dog. It was one of Jack Huff's helpers. The fellow told me that Will and Jack could not get along together, so Will had left for his home. I let the man chain and take Smoky Jack. The dog looked pathetically over his shoulder a couple of times as I stood there in front of my tent. I thought I could see by the look in his eye that he thought I had betrayed him.

A few days after this, I led a party of men and women to the top of Mount Le Conte where we were to spend the night before returning the next day. I found Smoky Jack chained to his kennel and without a nearby pan of water. I asked Jack Huff about it and he told me that they had to keep the dog chained to prevent his escape. I said, "Well, let's let him loose while I am up here. You know he is not going to leave me." I reached down and unsnapped the chain. The dog was overjoyed. He had already barked as we entered the camp. He ran down to the spring and got a drink of water. He then came back and stayed close to me. The party I had guided wanted to see the sunset from Cliff Top. Jack went with us and lay down close to me while we sat and watched a beautiful, golden sunset. I took him to his kennel after feeding him and told him to "stay."

I arose the next morning to make coffee for my clients before we walked out to Myrtle Point to see a gorgeous sunrise. It seemed like old times when we walked out to the point that morning—Jack running ahead of me, then turning and coming back because he thought we were too slow or hesitated along the trail too long.

After breakfast I asked Jack Huff to chain the dog since my party wished to hike back down the mountain. He did. I dared not look around after I asked Jack to do this, for I knew too well the dog would be wondering why he could not go along with his master. Before leaving, I again asked Jack to keep a pan of water near the dog at all times so he could drink when he desired. It seemed to me that Smoky Jack was a little thinner than the last time I saw him, but I did not think too much about it.

A few days after this, I met Will Ramsey on the road between the store and hotel. As we saw each other, there seemed to be a strange, not-too-friendly atmosphere. I greeted him as I normally did when we met, but I felt there was something wrong. I said, "Will, what is the matter with you? Have I done something to you?"

He said, "No, Paul, you haven't done a thing to me, I have no hard feelings against you at all. But Jack Huff and I couldn't get along, so I moved out, thinking that I could do guide work again for the hotel and other people who come to Gatlinburg. Andy told me he has hired a guide at the hotel now who has his preference and I would have to talk to him about work."

I smiled and said, "Why, Will, who am I to take any of your former patrons away from you? If people prefer you, they are welcome to you."

I asked about Smoky Jack. Will told me he and Jack Huff had had a talk about the dog. He thought the dog would be taken care of properly but that he would not go to the store and back by himself as he had done for me. He had to be chained by the individual who brought him down. Otherwise, the dog would slip away and look me up and he always found me regardless of where I was. He had to be chained all the time on the mountain. I did not particularly like that but, if he were going to be away from me, he would have to be chained.

A few days after this, I was sitting on the front porch of the hotel conversing with members of the Smoky Mountains Hiking Club, who were waiting to eat supper before returning to Knoxville. They said Smoky Jack was being abused on top of Mount Le Conte. Several people pointed out that, if I thought anything at all of him, I would get Jack away from there because his spirit was being broken. I could not believe their warnings.

That week I had another party to guide to the top of Mount Le Conte. When we had climbed to a spot just below Rainbow Falls, we noticed that coming down the trail was a man accompanying Smoky Jack with his saddle pockets on. Jack rushed to me and barked happily. I reached down and petted him as he walked around me. The man who was with him spoke to all of us. The dog would not go on with him, so it was I who snapped a chain which was in the saddle pockets to his collar and sent him on.

My party and I continued our way on up the mountain. We arrived at the top and were sitting around drinking coffee at one of the camp tables when Jack came bounding into camp alone. He came into camp at least an hour before the man who was taking him down that morning. He told me later that he had had to keep the dog chained all the way down to the store and while the packs were being loaded he had to chain Smoky Jack to one of the porch's upright posts. When they started back up the mountain, the dog was pulling hard on his chain. He told me, "I couldn't carry my pack and hold that dog, Paul, I just couldn't do it.

I knew that you were up here someplace, so I cut the dog loose. Before I could tuck his chain into the saddle pockets, the dog had disappeared. He wouldn't pay attention to my voice at all. He knew that you were up here, too, and wanted to reach you."

I told the fellow that the dog came in a good hour before he had arrived and that I had taken the saddle pockets off. Their weight was exactly thirty pounds. I fed the dog a few scraps of food I found around the camp and he went to the spring happily satisfied that he was again with his master. Huff and Ramsey apparently never bought him dog biscuits. (I always saw to it that Jack was rewarded after bringing supplies into camp.)

All the workers on the cabin and elsewhere in the camp knew that Smoky Jack did not have to be chained while I was there. I think that, if the truth were known, the dog was treated unkindly by some of the workers. I noticed this particular time that there were three with whom the dog would not associate. I wondered why. The dog followed me around closely and would not let me out of his sight. He seemed happy while I was in camp. When we got ready to leave the following morning, it was Jack Huff who chained him.

A couple of nights after this, the dog came to the hotel grounds and found me asleep. He did not awaken me this time as he always had before. He was lying on a rug beside my cot when I arose the next morning. He greeted me as he normally did. Again, I let the man come and get the dog but told him that I had been hearing tales of abuse to Jack from those who had visited the camp. The man assured me that the dog was never overpacked and that, aside from being chained, he was fed only by Huff and used every other day to bring supplies to camp. The fellow did, however, want to know when that party from Chicago was going to climb the mountain. How had he learned of the pending visit I do not know. He seemed to know that a rather large party was coming in from that city, some of whom had climbed Mount Le Conte the previous year. He also knew that I would be guiding them to the top of the mountain.

The Chicagoans arrived in Gatlinburg late that afternoon. After resting over the first day, they decided that they wanted to go to the top of

Mount Le Conte from the Alum Cave side, spend one night there, then come down and spend one night at the Grassy Patch Cabin, if weather permitted outside sleeping. There were twenty men and women in the group. I told them that we would need additional help to carry as much food as possible with us. I hired Will Ramsey to accompany us. He had been with some of the party the year before and they liked him.

The next morning, taxicabs took the party to Dave Ogle's store in the upper part of the Sugarlands. We made the hike up to the Grassy Patch Cabin where we left a part of our food, our sleeping bags, and our blankets. We were at Alum Cave before lunch. These were all seasoned hikers, so we did not dilly-dally along on the climb. We arrived in camp about two o'clock in the afternoon.

Smoky Jack was not in camp. Examining his quarters, I found that his chain was there. We found out from one of Huff's helpers that the dog had been taken down the mountain late that morning to help bring supplies from Gatlinburg.

We were sitting around in the camp on benches, drinking coffee and other beverages before walking out to Myrtle Point to view the vast mountainous areas spread out below us. Will and I had placed our food supplies in lockers. Suddenly he told me to look down the Le Conte Creek Trail. I saw Smoky Jack leading a man up the mountain. The dog was chained and was attempting to walk a little ahead of the fellow who had a firm hold on the chain. Talk of a swaybacked horse! Jack was certainly swaybacked from the weight of his pack.

As Jack came into camp, he smelled my scent and tried to run toward me. He could not because of the pack's weight. The man jerked hard on the chain when the dog attempted to run and jerked him off his feet. He then looked our way to see what made the dog try to run. He saw me standing there. He had already drawn one foot back to kick the dog while the animal was attempting to regain his footing. The kick was never delivered. They both walked on up to where I was standing near a food locker. I was reaching down to unchain the dog when the man said, "Don't do that!"

I must have been red in the face from what Will told me later. I said, "He's my dog, and I'll do what I damn well please with him."

"You leave him alone!"

This fellow then rushed to take the saddle pockets off the dog, but I was already unfastening the bellyband. The man did not like this and plainly showed his displeasure. He reached for the saddle pockets a second time and again I had to tell him that I would take them off. The dog, when I released my hand from his belt, dropped right at my feet. Will Ramsey was standing near me. He looked at me, I at him. He said, "Paul, hold your temper. Hold your temper."

Those saddle pockets weighed so much that it took both hands for me to lift them off the dog. Normally, I lifted them off with just one hand by taking hold of the middle part. These were heavy, very heavy, containing much more than the thirty-pound limit I had imposed. I walked over and got the hoist scale I had brought the year before. I carried the scales back and hung the ring on a large nail driven into a tree. I lifted the pockets onto the scale hook. They weighed forty-seven pounds. Huff's helper said the scale was wrong and that the dog could bring in twice that weight.

I told the fellow that the scales were correct. It was he who was wrong.

I was fairly sure that he had been told not to pack the dog with more than thirty pounds. I told him that even Charlie Ogle had said the dog was overpacked at times, that I had been doing a little inquiring myself as to the dog's treatment, and that I was not going to stand for any more of it.

I had Will and a couple of the husky men in our party lift the saddle pockets and they said the weight was between forty and fifty pounds. No wonder the dog was so exhausted! Will looked at me out of the corner of his eye. He knew good and well that Smoky Jack would be accompanying us down the mountain the next day.

Our party was ready to go to Myrtle Point. I did not encourage the dog to go with us, but I did tell the two men in camp not to chain him. He would not leave as long as I was nearby. About twenty-five minutes after we had reached the spot and while Will and I were pointing out the distant peaks to our party, Jack appeared. He laid down at my feet and put his head across my lap. It seemed that he was still exhausted. He was thin, too. I did not like that. I petted him on the head and neck as he lay there and he weakly wagged his tail. He was reluctant to leave my side. When we walked back across Maintop and into camp, he heeled of his own accord. I could plainly see that his spirit was slowly being broken.

That night when we went to bed, I took Jack down to his kennel and told him to go to bed. Talking to him softly, I said, "Jack, you and I are going off this mountain together tomorrow. You don't have to work up here anymore. I'm taking you home."

The next morning, when Will and I arose to make coffee for the hikers before walking out to Myrtle Point to see the sunrise, Smoky Jack was lying on the bare ground just outside the closed cabin. Evidently he had slept outside the door of the cabin all night.

As I led the party out to see the sunrise, Smoky Jack accompanied us. He seemed to be more like his old self. At times, he strayed into the woods. We did not tarry long at the point and made our way back into camp soon after the sun had risen. Will had breakfast ready and we ate heartily. I fed the dog and every bite or so he took, he would stop and look up at me as I watched him.

As Will packed our remaining food to be carried off the mountain, I walked over to Huff's personal section of the camp and asked for Jack's saddle pockets and chain. Huff said, "Oh, leave him here, Paul. We'll never pack him that heavy again. We'll keep his pack within the thirty-pound limit."

I answered, "No, I've been hearing tales about his treatment up here. Yesterday I made up my mind that he had carried his last load to camp. I'm taking him off the mountain."

One of Huff's men interrupted and said, "We have to keep him chained all the time, Paul, otherwise he slips his collar and goes to you. We had to cure him of swelling his neck by tightening his collar."

I replied, "Yes, I have heard about that, too. Look at the collar. It's been fastened in the fifth notch and the tightness is choking the dog. He can't get his breath. No, there's no use arguing about the matter. I've made up my mind to take him off the mountain with me."

Huff went to one of the lockers for Jack's saddle pockets. I strapped them on him, putting the cow chain in one pocket and the lead chain in the other. The two of us then joined the hiking party. Most of them were watching us and talking softly to Will Ramsey as we approached. I asked them if they had settled their account with Huff, and they said they had. I said, "Let's get started down the mountain."

We had a very happy dog along with us. Smoky Jack seemed unusually happy. He would run ahead of us a little way and then come rushing back toward us. Sometimes he would look back over his shoulder at me when we were in the lead. Will remarked several times that the dog seemed happier than he had seen him in several weeks.

He had a right to be. We were together again.

But he did not know what still lay ahead.

CHAPTER FOURTEEN

Down Mount Le Conte

Smoky Jack was a happy dog the morning he accompanied us down the Alum Cave Trail from the top of Mount Le Conte. We took our time going down to Grassy Patch Cabin to spend the night before our return to Gatlinburg on the third day.

Will Ramsey had told the group that when Smoky Jack had his saddle pockets on, he was "all business" and that no one should try to pet him. While we hiked, no one tried to touch him.

Vegetation in the higher altitudes was a great deal different than in the valleys and Will and I identified many trees, shrubs, and wildflowers for the hikers. Will's names for plants were different from mine. He knew the mountain names for the plants and I knew both the common names and the botanical ones. I identified birds, too, and both of us talked about the animals we saw. Smoky Jack was perfectly content and quiet.

Jack was ahead of us when we came to the abrupt left-hand turn of the trail on top of the ridge. The man leading called to me to say that the

dog did not want him to go around and on out the ridge. I called back and told him that the dog knew what he was doing. This was where we made the abrupt turn onto the rocks and I said that it would be best to wait there until Will and I arrived to help the party down to Alum Cave.

I led the way over the treacherous rocks with Smoky Jack running ahead. We had little difficulty getting our party down to the cave. There I took off Jack's saddle pockets. He was friendly with everyone. They could run their hands over him and pet him and one lady found out he knew how to shake hands. Several tried to get the dog to accept food from them, but he would sniff at it and would not eat it. One lady, after the dog had smelled a piece of bread and did not accept it from her hand, threw it on the ground, thinking perhaps the dog would pick it up and eat it. To her surprise, he walked away from it.

GRASSY PATCH CABIN. THOMPSON BROTHERS DIGITAL PHOTOGRAPH COLLECTION, UNIVERSITY OF TENNESSEE, KNOXVILLE LIBRARIES.

Will thought he would have a little fun and called Jack over and gave him a scrap of bread. The dog took it and ate it. This caused raised eyebrows among the group. Another lady called the dog to her to offer him a piece of meat. Jack sniffed at it a long time but refused to touch it. He looked at me. I did not move, so he backed away. The lady asked, "Mr. Adams, do you have this dog trained not to accept food from strangers?" I smiled as I told the dog to take the meat. He brought it to me and laid it in my outstretched hand. I looked at it, examined it, and handed it back to him. He ate it.

After lunch the party separated. Will led three men on down to the creek below us to fish for rainbow and speckled trout while I led the rest of the party down the trail to the Grassy Patch Cabin.

We were lucky that afternoon to find a nest of the black-throated blue warblers in a thicket near the cabin. I had usually been able to find here one or two nests of this bird in nesting season. I got down on my hands and knees and crawled around until I discovered a nest, then called the hikers over to see the daintily constructed nest. We did not disturb the eggs or bother the parent birds.

When we arrived at Grassy Patch Cabin, Smoky Jack felt right at home. He had been here many times before with me. I removed the saddle pockets and let Jack have the run of the place. Smoky Jack would jump about, howl a little, run from me and then back because he was so glad to be with me again.

Will and three fishermen came in about an hour before sunset with more than forty speckled trout. Will and I cleaned the catch and prepared supper. There were enough trout for all of us to have generous portions. We relished the delicious treat.

After supper, we went down to the creek bank and started a fire. Here, with Jack lying close to me, we sat around the fire as Will and I entertained with stories of the Great Smokies. We told of the large balds of Thunderhead and Gregory and Parson, of Cades Cove and its inhabitants, and of the Chilhowee Mountains. We were questioned about the North Carolina side. Will told them of my friendship with Kephart, the famous outdoor writer who lived in Bryson City, and how I had hunted and fished with him on Hazel Creek. There were many questions about this naturalist.

After the fire had been replenished several times and we ran out of wood to feed it, we walked back to the cabin. The men and women dispersed into their sleeping quarters, a few on the outside of the cabin, some on the inside. Before Will and I retired, we walked back down to the fire to make sure that the dying embers were out. Smoky Jack followed. Will asked me what I was going to do with the dog. He said he, too, was attached to him. I told him that in all probability I would take him into Knoxville to be cared for by my mother and sister.

Will asked, "Why don't you let me keep him, Paul? I'll be good to him and he is an added attraction to hikers in the mountains now. He gets along fine with my dogs and, besides that, I don't live quite as far away from the hotel as Charlie Ogle. Jack will be a lot closer to you when you want to pack him into the mountains. Let him stay with me, Paul. We might need him if hikers get lost. We can use him in trailing them."

I never could argue much with Will. He and I had the same opinions about many things. We were very congenial. I knew that Smoky Jack would be happier here in the mountains than confined to a house in Knoxville and exercised only once or twice a day. I accepted Will's suggestion.

After breakfast the next day, we started back down the old road toward Dave Ogle's store. From Grassy Patch, I carried the dog's saddle pockets in my almost-empty packsack so Jack could run free. Our hike of nearly four miles was made leisurely since we had plenty of time. We arrived at the hotel in time for lunch. Andy Huff was standing on the hotel porch watching the taxicabs unload their customers. He saw us get out. I reached into Jack's saddle pockets and withdrew the chain to snap onto the dog's collar. I handed the chain to Will and told the dog to go along with him. The two of them walked up Glades Road toward Will's home.

Andy said to me, "Paul, I heard that you brought Smoky Jack off the mountain yesterday. I don't blame you a bit for that. I knew he was being abused up there on the mountain. But I definitely don't want you to keep him here on the hotel grounds."

I let Andy unwind then told him that Jack would stay at Will Ramsey's. Perhaps we would use him in some of our hikes and trips up the mountain from Gatlinburg.

I said, "Yes, I made a big mistake by letting the dog stay up there after Will left the top of the mountain. I'll never do such a thing again. But have no fear about his staying here. Will and I both will see that he's no problem."

That afternoon, I put on my bathing suit and walked down to the swimming hole below the mouth of Roaring Fork Creek. There I found other swimmers. I knew most of them. My friends asked if it were true that I had brought Smoky Jack off Mount Le Conte. News travels fast in the mountains by mouth to ear. They also wanted to know if I was going to take the dog into Knoxville or keep him in Gatlinburg. I told them that I would keep him handy to make guiding trips with me. Everyone seemed to like the idea and said it would seem strange to them to see me walking along the roads without my dog.

Smoky Jack seemed to be content at Will Ramsey's, although he had to be chained most of the time. Once in a while he would slip his collar at night and come to my tent, only to be taken back to Will's the next morning before breakfast. He seemed to enjoy these morning runs. Sometimes when Will had to come into town to buy groceries, he would be accompanied by the loose-running dog. Smoky Jack would usually come through the hotel yard and smell around the tent. If I was not there, he would go back to Will and follow him or run along in front of him. Jack soon learned that his Gatlinburg home was with Will Ramsey.

CHAPTER FIFTEEN

Smoky Jack to the Rescue

Smoky Jack and I played important roles in each other's lives the remainder of that summer of 1926. Many people had heard about the dog and wished to make his acquaintance, so I took him along on most of my guiding trips. There were several times when he went on hikes with Will and his parties.

I was asked by Dr. Harry Jennison[37] of the University of Tennessee to guide into the mountains a busload of students from the University of Kansas. This group was part of the College on Wheels program where

---

37. Harry M. Jennison (1885–1940) was a professor of botany at the University of Tennessee and an expert on the flora of the Great Smoky Mountains. He was president (1930–31) of the Smoky Mountains Hiking Club and secretary of the Great Smoky Mountains Conservation Association.

students were given college credit for study in various parts of the United States. The students were chaperoned by a faculty member and his wife.

At the same time, there were members of the Prairie Hiking Club from Chicago camped in Gatlinburg. I was supposed to be a constant guide for these hikers. There were others staying at the hotel from near Washington, D.C., and New York City who wished to use me as chief guide. All three of these groups were in Gatlinburg at the same time. I felt I had to be attentive to each group and guide them where they wanted to go.

The week before these three parties arrived in Gatlinburg, I noticed quite a bit of activity around the old mill. On the front of the building was placed a sign, "Tea Room." Mrs. Ben Barbee, who was the new proprietor, had purchased the old Gatlinburg Water Mill which had not been used for years. The mill stood on the north side of Roaring Fork Creek, near its mouth. A house known as the Wiley Oakley house stood opposite the mill, on the south side of the creek. The main road, Highway 66, between Gatlinburg and Sevierville passed in front of both buildings.

One day I found Mrs. Barbee standing in the mill's parking area. She asked me to come in and look over things. I told her I could not stop right then but promised to come down later and visit with her and her daughter, Leland, and son, Ben. I came back and ate supper with the Barbees and had a nice visit with them. They wanted to know all about Smoky Jack. None of them had met him, but they had read in the Knoxville newspapers of our activities together and were anxious to meet him. I told them that I would bring him down the next day to be formally introduced.

They took a liking to Smoky Jack and he to them. They suggested that I let him stay there with them, but I refused, saying that a great many people were afraid of large dogs and would not patronize places where there was one as big as Smoky Jack. However, during the course of the summer, Smoky Jack and I did appear quite often in the mill's Tea Room particularly if the party I was guiding returned to Gatlinburg after the hotel's supper hour.

The day after the Prairie Hiking Club established its camp on the island,[38] I was asked to guide several members to the top of Mount Le Conte on an overnight hike. Smoky Jack went with us, packing some of our food supplies. The group rode to Cherokee Orchard in taxi-cabs. Smoky Jack and I walked, starting a little earlier. The hike up the mountain was uneventful. We made it in good time, eating our lunches at Rainbow Falls and afterward hiking on up to the camp. Smoky Jack and I took them out to Myrtle Point and to Cliff Top. The next morning, we were up early and walked out to Myrtle Point to see the sunrise. When it was time for us to descend, I asked one of the leaders if it would be all right for me to bring up the rear. There were some bird nests out on Maintop and Cliff Top which I had been observing and I wanted to revisit these sites before starting down.

After getting the hikers started down the mountain, Smoky Jack and I hiked back to Maintop. I observed nests of the red-breasted nuthatch, junco, and winter wren and two nests of veeries which I had previously found. I wrote notes to be transferred later into my journals. I followed the ridge trail over to Cliff Top and then came back through camp to drink a cup of coffee before starting down the mountain. When I found nests inside of pecked-out holes, I had an unusual method of observing the eggs and young. I carried a small mirror with a six-inch handle on it. This could be attached to a long stick if the nest was above my head. Then, with the beam of a flashlight pointed against the mirror, its reflection would allow me to observe what was at the bottom of the hole. The parent birds did not particularly like this, but they tolerated it. I would stand there and write down my observations.

Perhaps two hours elapsed from the time I left the camp until I returned. There sat two girls from the Prairie Hiking Club waiting for me. They were close friends and had attended the same private school in

---

38. The island referred to is a large plot of dry ground in the middle of the Little Pigeon River that was used as a farm field and later as a campground. The island is immediately across the river from the Pi Beta Phi Settlement School grounds.

Chicago. I had seen them start down the mountain with the rest of the party, but they had not gone far until they decided to go back to camp and wait for me. I had left Smoky Jack's saddle pockets in camp when the two of us started upon our private excursion. By hiking quickly down the mountain, I had planned to catch up with the group of hikers between Rainbow Falls and the Orchard. I fussed at the girls for act-ing foolishly, then I strapped Jack's saddle pockets on and we started down the trail. The girls had to be helped through the long rock bar and around Rainbow Falls. It took us three hours to make the descent. Smoky Jack and I would have made it in a little over an hour. We did not stop to make observations of plants and animals on our way down for we were walking against time. The sun was setting.

When we arrived at the Orchard, Jim Huff was sitting in his taxicab waiting for us. He said to me, "Your name is *mud* with the mother of one of these girls. She is going to bless you out when you arrive at the island."

I told Jim why we were late. When we arrived at the island, the girl's mother was not there, so I could offer no explanation. Jim took me back to Will's house where I chained Jack.

Knowing that supper had been served, I changed into street clothes and went down to the Tea Room and ordered my meal. Mrs. Barbee came out of the kitchen soon after I was served and sat down at my table. It seemed that the discussed mother of one of the girls had become quite fond of Mrs. Barbee and often visited her. After her daughter and friend had failed to show up with the rest of the group, the mother had gone to the Tea Room. She was afraid that her daughter and friend had been kept on the mountain by a "strange guide" for immoral purposes. Mrs. Barbee let her unwind and then, placing her hands on her hips, told the girl's mother that she trusted me more in the woods than she trusted herself with her own children. She also told the mother that we would turn up sooner or later and that the girls would not have been molested in any way. This seemed to relieve the mother, who then walked back to her camp.

Smoky Jack and I hiked back up to the top of Mount Le Conte the next day with the party from the East. At their request, the dog was taken along. This group had heard of him and they wanted to see him scale the bluff around Rainbow Falls. They wanted to watch him go through the long rock bar and take the shortcuts he had made where hikers could not follow because of the steep slopes. Most of them wanted pictures of him doing these things. This was another overnight hike.

The afternoon we came down, Andy Huff told me that the College on Wheels leaders were looking for me. They wanted to climb Mount Le Conte the next day. The group was camped just above the Riverside Hotel, about half a mile from Ogle's Store. I walked up to their campsite and talked with the students and their leaders. They wanted me to take Smoky Jack along. While there, several of the students asked me to give them the scientific names of plants they had collected along the river bank and were pressing for reports. Smoky Jack and I returned to their camp about seven the next morning. Because the students wanted to continue their nature studies, the hike up to the top of Mount Le Conte consumed most of the day. We made many stops and gathered around their chaperones, both of whom were botanists. I think about a third of the plant species we looked at and studied were familiar to the students; the others I had to identify or help them "key out." We arrived in camp before sundown. After supper, we walked to Cliff Top to see a glorious sunset and were back in camp before dark.

Our hike down the mountain the next day was slow, but I returned the hikers to their bus by dark. I was relieved that the following day was Sunday. I was tired and could relax before I had to be on the trails again Monday with a group from the Prairie Hiking Club. Smoky Jack came to my tent Saturday night, but before anyone was stirring around the hotel Sunday morning I had taken him back to Will's. I lolled around the hotel most of the morning, then found Colonel and Mrs. Chapman, together with Mr. and Mrs. W. P. Davis,[39] sitting on the hotel porch waiting for lunch.

---

39. Willis P. Davis was a manager of Knoxville Iron Company and a member of the Boards of Directors of the Knoxville Chamber of Commerce and the Knoxville Automobile Club. He and his wife, Anne, were early advocates for a national park in the Great Smoky Mountains.

They wanted to know if I was keeping busy in my new position. I told them that I had made three trips to and from the top of Mount Le Conte during the past week and that I was content as a nature guide. After a few minutes, the colonel rose from his chair and asked me to accompany him into the yard where we could talk in private.

I knew he had something on his mind. He told me that those on the camp committee of the Conservation Association were sorry they had not left me on the mountain for this season, that the Champion Fibre Company had terminated its agreement with the Association and placed the camp under new management, and that the Association had lost money on the deal.

I told the colonel that I was aware of the situation on Mount Le Conte and followed it since the beginning of the "house-that-Jack-built." I also told him that I was present when Jack Huff had told Lewis McCarter to stay off the top of the mountain and take care of the lower part only. Huff had said he would take care of the upper part and do what he pleased up there. The colonel asked why I had not informed him that a larger cabin or lodge was being built. I said that I had thought of reporting the construction job but I did not think it would help my position with them so said nothing about it.

When the Chapmans and Davises were called to lunch, the colonel insisted that I eat with them in the main dining room. The five of us

HIKERS AT JACK HUFF'S LE CONTE LODGE. ALBERT "DUTCH" ROTH IN CENTER. JIM THOMPSON, PHOTOGRAPHER. THOMPSON BROTHERS DIGITAL PHOTOGRAPH COLLECTION, UNIVERSITY OF TENNESSEE, KNOXVILLE LIBRARIES.

shared a very pleasant meal. Mrs. Chapman, who owned a white German police dog, wanted to know about Smoky Jack and I told her he was being kept at Will Ramsey's home.

On Monday morning, I led a part of the Prairie Hiking Club up the old Indian Gap Trail and back. It was an all-day hike and gave the club members a different understanding of the valleys in the mountains. A mile above Dave Ogle's store, we were in virgin forest. The transition to different species of trees and shrubs as we gained altitude was noticed by all. It was a delightful day for hiking above the three thousand-foot elevation. We ate our lunches in Indian Gap.

We retraced our steps along the same route we had taken up the valley and did not arrive at the College on Wheels group camp until nearly dark. Here I was informed that five students had become separated from a larger group about noon and had not returned. The professor and his wife were beginning to worry. They wanted a search party organized. I offered to go on into Gatlinburg and try to find some men to go with us. If the students had not returned by the time I got back to their camp, we would start a search. I then asked him to get some of the students' clothing—preferably unwashed socks or stockings—put them in a paper sack and close the sack tightly so that no odor could be smelled through it.

The members of the Prairie Hiking Club offered to go with me, but I was confident that Smoky Jack would find the five missing students. Armed with the paper sack, I returned to Gatlinburg. Smoky Jack and I walked to the kitchen of the hotel where Mary was washing dishes. I asked her to prepare some lunches since I knew the lost had not eaten since noon. I outlined the situation to her and said that I would walk on up the Glades Road and get Will Ramsey and Marshall Ogle to join the search party.

Andy Huff walked into the kitchen and he told me that he would send his son Jim after Will and Marshall. He suggested that I sit down and eat a late supper and wash my feet and change my socks. I went to my tent and did as he suggested. I also put a first-aid kit and flashlight into my packsack. I walked back to the kitchen for a late supper. Smoky Jack was fed just outside the kitchen door. As I finished my meal, Will and Marshall arrived.

We called Smoky Jack and drove back to the College on Wheels campground. Here we listened to the students as they gave us directions to the spot where the students had become separated from the group. (About a dozen students, without a guide, had gone to Alum Cave. It was above the cave that the five had become separated.)

There was speculation as to whether these students had actually gone to the top of Mount Le Conte or had followed the indistinct trail across Peregrine Peak and then had run out of trail and started down through the timber to a stream and tried to follow that back to some road.

The professor and three students insisted that they would go along with us. I had to refuse their help. Marshall, Will, and I knew tracking would be rough and we also knew it was better to have only two or three persons with a trailing dog. Trailing dogs do not like to have a "crowd" behind them. It disturbs their work.

The three of us and Jack drove to a spot near Dave Ogle's store, then we walked up the old Indian Gap Road. We decided our best bet was to go up the Bearpen Hollow Trail half a mile and let the dog smell the socks in the paper sack. Jack scented the ground. There was no sign of them here, so we kept climbing. We were another half-mile above when Smoky Jack stopped suddenly and lifted his nose into the air. The dog barked loud and clear. He left the trail and pulled toward the east. We followed. We crossed a steep hollow then went to the top of a ridge. Here the dog again barked loud and clear. We were getting closer to our quarry. But where were they?

Will and Marshall had been quiet after I let the dog smell the socks and both kept close behind Smoky Jack and me. We were hiking through dark woods, each with a flashlight. It was all I could do to hold onto the dog through the dark woods and around house-sized boulders. The three of us were stumbling along, trying to keep up with Jack.

Finally I said, "Let's be quiet for just a few moments and listen the best we can and look eastward." I then said to the dog, "Speak, Jack, speak." He spoke—two very loud barks followed closely by a sort of wailing howl. Then he was quiet. All of us listened. We did not hear an answering call. After a few moments, we decided to follow the dog again. We went across another hollow and up a steep grade to the top of another ridge. Here I reined in the dog and told him to keep quiet. We all listened again, but we heard nothing.

I asked Jack to speak again. This time an answering "hello" came from below us. The dog gave a strong lurch in that direction. I held him back. Will, who was the best yodeler, answered the calls.

I called loud and slowly, "Stay where you are. We are coming to you." A member of the party answered affirmative. Straining at his leash, Jack led us to them. We were going downhill now but still had one small ridge to cross.

Then we found the three boys and two girls huddled together on the lower side of a large boulder. It was after midnight. All of them were cold and most of them had scratches. Otherwise, they were all right! There was not a match in the party, so they had not made a campfire. None of them had an outer jacket. Darkness had caught them before they could find a creek from which to quench their thirst.

Marshall quickly made a fire. They all huddled around it, each trying to absorb the heat. As they huddled around the campfire, the lost hikers told us that, after climbing as high as Echo Point on top of Alum Cave ridge, they had become separated from the rest of the group. When they reached the indistinct place where the trail turned abruptly left, they became bewildered. They started down, but they did not recognize the almost smooth steep area they had climbed that morning. After deciding they had not come to the top of the Alum Cave this way, they climbed back to the top of the ridge and walked back and forth on it for more than an hour looking for a place to descend. When they could not find a way down, they decided the best way to get off the ridge was to hike through the woods on the right-hand side and follow a ravine until they came to a stream they could see in the distance.

That was their mistake. The walking was rough and slow. From the ridge they could not see the large boulders and tall trees they would have to go around. Growth on top of the ridge was scrubby and thick. They had not bargained on running into so many rhododendron thickets and gigantic rocks they had to work around. They had started down the ravine but, before they found water, darkness caught them in an almost impenetrable forest.

After they were reasonably warm and had eaten the food and drunk the hot coffee and hot chocolate, we put out the fire. Then with everyone carrying a flashlight and Jack running free again, we made our way back to the Bearpen Hollow Trail. Will Ramsey led the way, but the trip took a good hour since we had to walk around gigantic rocks and large trees.

Daylight was breaking when we arrived at my car. All piled into it, even Jack. The going downhill was slow because of the rough road. The trip back to camp took another hour.

All the students and professors were preparing breakfast when we drove into camp. This was their day to travel toward the Roan Mountain section, then on to Washington, D.C., and on up the Maine coast. The professor insisted that we stay and have breakfast with them. Besides, he wanted me to give the whole group a firm lecture on getting off trails and not sticking together in unknown territory. Will thought it might do them some good. As soon as breakfast was over, the professor called all the students together and told them the five students would have to pay for the search party and for the help of the trailing dog.

There was a fantastic coincidence in this search. I had gone hunting for my own cousin! Soon after the professor settled up the bill, a young lady approached and asked if I was the son of Reverend Clair S. Adams of Knoxville. I answered that I was. She then said, "We are related. We're third cousins. I'm the daughter of Chan Adams of Atchison, Kansas." She seemed happy to meet one of her cousins whom she had heard about but never seen.

When we arrived back at the hotel, I told Will that I had to lead some hikers over to Norton Creek to see the large yellow poplars. He said, "You need some rest, Paul. Let Marshall and me walk home, and we will take Smoky Jack with us. You don't have to drive up there just to take us." I walked into the hotel kitchen where I found Andy. I told him that the lost had been found. He looked at me and said, "My God, Paul, you look tired! Go lie down. I'll go into the dining room and ask this party if they'd just as soon make the walk this afternoon instead of this morning."

I went to my tent and lay down after washing my feet and face and hands. I was so tired that I slept fitfully, reliving the trailing experience in my dreams.

About noon, I got up and dressed. I felt better. By one o'clock the hotel party and I were on our way to Norton Creek, walking leisurely. As we walked, I mentioned the names of plants they had seen but did not recognize. We arrived back at the hotel before supper.

After supper, I sat on the porch of the hotel and visited until dark before walking to my tent. I had just undressed and lain down on my cot when I heard voices of Andy and his son Jim outside the tent. I told them to come in. It seemed that two small boys at Elkmont were lost on the far side of Sugarland Mountain and search parties were being organized to look for them. They wanted my dog to participate in the search. Andy told me that the boy's parents were friends of his. I knew them, too. I said I wanted to go, so I got up and dressed. Andy and Jim walked back to the hotel to telephone Elkmont to tell the searchers that I would meet them in Fighting Creek Gap within the hour. I drove up to Will's and got Smoky Jack and his leash. Will told me that he would go, but I reminded him that he had a guiding trip the next day and suggested he had better get some rest. He came right back at me, saying that I also had a guiding trip. But after he learned that I would be accompanied by some Elkmont people, he decided not to go.

I returned to the hotel and packed everything I thought I would need, plus some food, and drove to Fighting Creek Gap. There must have been a dozen men standing near their cars waiting for us. They all wanted to go. "Two of you will be enough," I said. One man stepped forward, then another. I had previously asked Andy to tell them to bring a sock to the gap. They had forgotten all about it in their excitement.

We put Jack on the leash and started up the well-defined trail. Not too far up Sugarland, we found small footprints. I had Smoky Jack smell them. Shortly after we "topped-out" on Sugarland and started through a fenced-in area, the dog hesitated, smelled around the ground, and then took off along the fence. I encouraged Jack to follow the scent. As Smoky Jack and I walked around the fence, I told him that these were the tracks we were supposed to be following. He would wag his tail as I talked.

He was on the right trail now. He had picked up the scent we wanted him to follow.

At Huskey Gap where several trails crossed each other, the dog became somewhat confused. We wondered if the boys had walked up the ridge toward the Chimneys and Mount Collins or if they had taken the trail which led into the Little River area and to the old railroad grade along that stream. Here we had to make a choice in direction for the dog to trail. We decided that we should let Jack trail toward the Chimneys. He had gone about a quarter of a mile when he came to a complete stop, turned around, and looked at me, as if to say, "This is the end of their trail. They have gone no farther."

We retraced our steps to Huskey Gap and let Jack follow the other scent down the mountain. He was pulling hard on his leash as we descended. As we turned right along the old railroad bed, he started to pick up speed. Soon we were in Elkmont, in front of a darkened cottage. We woke the residents.

They had found the boys within an hour and a half after the three of us and Jack had left Fighting Creek Gap. All search parties had been called off except ours. I was puzzled. Why had they not sent word to us at Huskey Gap which they knew we had to cross if the dog worked properly? One of the men with us offered to take Smoky Jack and me to my car at Fighting Creek Gap. We were back in Gatlinburg by one o'clock in the morning. I took the dog to Will's and chained him, bidding him goodbye.

I returned quietly to the hotel, but Andy Huff heard me. Inviting him in to have a chair, I told him the whole story. When I had finished, he asked me if I had been paid for the use of the dog. I told him that I had not even been thanked, let alone been paid!

He said to me, "You send the boys' parents a bill for $50.00. I'll see that you get it."

I slept the remainder of the night and woke the following morning feeling refreshed. Smoky Jack went with Will that day on a one-day hike to the top of Mount Le Conte. I took a party to the top of Bullhead.

I walked down to the Tea Room after supper for a visit. I had not been there very long when the mother of one of the Prairie Hiking Club members came in to say that her daughter and a friend had failed to return from a hike up Mount Le Conte. She was worried. From what she could gather from the rest of the party, the group had safely reached the top of the mountain but her daughter and her girlfriend had decided to come down through trailless forest accompanied by a boy from Knoxville, who was to lead them to Trillium Gap. Would I go looking for them? I agreed.

As Mrs. Barbee prepared food and a thermos filled with hot drinks, I calculated that the two girls and the boy had planned to hike down the ridge to Trillium Gap, go on down Roaring Fork Creek, strike an old road leading past Sherman Clabo's house,[40] and walk from there to Gatlinburg. It would be easier this time for me to walk than to drive.

I had to pass Will's on the way, so I stopped to get Jack. Will insisted on going along since he knew the territory better than I. He dressed and got his flashlight and we were soon on our way with Smoky Jack. We attached his leash when we arrived in Trillium Gap.

Here I brought out the girls' and boy's socks I had been given. Jack sniffed at them and smelled around on the ground. Never once did he wag his tail or bark. This rather surprised Will and me. Knowing that other small ridges came off the top of Mount Le Conte, we decided to walk up the main ridge, thinking the girls may have crossed it at some spot.

There was no trail into Trillium Gap from the Gatlinburg side, but Will and I knew how to get around the thickets of rhododendron on the ridge. About half a mile above Trillium Gap, Smoky Jack paused, wagged his tail, and barked. Will and I saw the imprints of three pairs of shoes. Jack led us off to the left toward Trillium Branch and Cannon Creek. We had not gone far before we came to freshly broken small trees and shrub branches. We knew we were on the right track.

Will said, "My God, Paul, if we have to go into that area, we will be all night finding them."

I replied, "We are going to follow these tracks, wherever Jack leads us, even into Porters Flat, but I don't think that we will have to go that far."

---

40. Sherman Clabo's house was the last house up Roaring Fork Creek. Clabo owned an old sled road through Black Spruce Flats that was incorporated into the lower end of Adams's early trail to Trillium Gap.

We walked on slowly. From Jack's actions, we knew we were going in the right direction. We saw where the three lost hikers had tried to skirt some of the rhododendron and laurel thickets. We had to crawl through one of them. We crossed a couple of ridges. In the distance below, we saw the light of a campfire.

We did not call. When we were less than a hundred yards from the fire, I reined in the dog and asked Will in a quiet voice to stand his ground. We could see what was going on around the campfire and could hear loud talking.

The two girls were huddled together. The boy was a short distance away.

He was threatening to leave them alone in the woods if they did not submit to his advances. He ran toward the girls.

That was when I turned Jack loose, unsnapping his leash and ordering him in a firm, low voice, "Charge!" It did not take him many bounds to enter the circle of the firelight. The girls recognized him at once. Smoky Jack went over and stood before the girls and snarled at the boy, showing his teeth as Will and I came into the fire's light.

One of the girls looked up at me and said with tears in her eyes, "Mr. Adams, we hoped you'd come! We have fended off this man for hours in these woods. He has threatened to leave us many times if we did not give in to him!" Then both girls burst into tears.

We gave all three of them food and hot chocolate or coffee. The boy, who had thought he could find his way down the mountain through a trackless forest, said little.

The girls told their story between bites of food. When they left Mount Le Conte, they had hiked down a small ridge leading into wilderness. They decided to try the ridge to their left, a larger and somewhat higher one they could see in the distance. Then they ran into an immense rhododendron thicket and, after they had moved around this, they thought they were on the correct ridge. After they left the main top of Mount Le Conte, clouds had begun to cover the sky. At dusk they did not know where they were so they took off down a hollow, knowing they would eventually come to water and could follow a stream. The hiking had become rougher and their climb down the hollow led them through more rhododendron and around large boulders. They camped at the first water they reached. They had matches with them, so they built a fire. Soon after dark had fallen, the boy started making improper advances. His conduct had been insulting for several hours.

Will led the way back into Trillium Gap. Each of us carried a flashlight. I made the boy bring up the rear and, when he tried to speak to me, I would tell him to shut up. I was already mad at him, so we would settle our difficulties and differences after we got the girls safely back to their camp.

The girls were tired and needed to rest frequently. When we came to the sled road above Sherman Clabo's cabin, we rested again. Will said to me, "Paul, why don't I hurry on down to Sherman's and borrow his horses for these girls to ride?" That was a good idea. He left immediately and I led the three lost hikers down after they had rested for another few minutes.

When we arrived at the cabin, Will and Sherman waited with two saddled horses. The young man asked where his horse was and Will told him off in no uncertain terms. Sherman also put in a few words. I was reserving his cussing out until later.

Within another hour, we had the girls at the Prairie Hiking Club camp. The boy left us near the hotel. After greeting the mother, who was relieved to know her daughter had not been harmed, Will and I mounted the horses and rode to my tent. Will took my horse and called Smoky Jack to follow him. The dog obediently went with him.

In the afternoon of the next day, I walked to the swimming hole. I was stopped by a taxicab driver who told me he had taken a young man into Sevierville that morning to catch a bus for Knoxville. The boy said he was afraid I was going to kill him. On their way into Sevierville, the young man gave his side of the hiking episode. The driver told the young fellow he did not think I would kill him but that I would certainly cuss him out in no uncertain terms.

CHAPTER SIXTEEN

End of an Era

Time ran on for Smoky Jack and me around Gatlinburg. He accompanied me several times as I guided groups to the top of Mount Le Conte. I also took him along when I guided parties over the state line to the Cherokee Indian Reservation in North Carolina. When we rode horseback, Jack did not carry his saddle pockets but was allowed to run free. I carried his lead chain from my saddle to keep it handy. During a trip across Indian Gap, our party often stayed at a boarding house in Smokemont. There we would eat supper and spend the night. The next day after breakfast we would go to Cherokee and return to Gatlinburg by nightfall. The boarding house owner allowed Smoky Jack to sleep in my room. The proprietor took quite a fancy to the dog and wanted to buy him, but I refused.

Early one morning, Andy Huff came to my tent and told me that the sheriff of Sevier County wanted Jack and me to go into the Porters Flat area to trail a man charged with murder. To my dismay, I knew the fugitive. I suggested that the sheriff send for the bloodhounds from Brushy Mountain State Prison. The sheriff had already made that request, but the bloodhounds were trailing in Sumner County. I told Andy that I had to guide a party that day and that neither the dog nor I was available. I had previously told Andy that I preferred the dog be used only when people visiting our settlement became lost and it became necessary to trail them.

As autumn approached, I was not as busy with guide work after Labor Day. People who had been vacationing in the mountains had left for their homes where children were to enter school. Temperatures had begun to drop and nights were much cooler. Weeks went by when there was no guide work at all. I realized I had to have another job with guiding as a sideline.

Sleeping in my tent on the hotel grounds was not to my satisfaction. Before Mrs. Barbee had taken her children back to Knoxville for the start of school, we had discussed the possibility of my living upstairs in the mill, if only to give some protection to the contents of her Tea Room and the mill's grounds. There was a cook stove in the kitchen of the nearby Wiley Oakley house and some household furniture which she said I could use. Consequently, after settling my account with Andy and striking my tent for the season, I moved to the Barbee property.

At first I lived in the upstairs of the old mill. Mrs. Barbee and her children returned once or twice a month on weekends, usually bringing my mother and sister to visit. For me to stay all winter in the mill would require putting up a stove and firing it quite heavily in order to keep warm. It was inconvenient for me to cook in the Oakley house then cross a footlog to the rear of both buildings to enter my sleeping quarters. It was therefore decided that I should move to the house and lock the mill, going into it occasionally to see if things were all right.

When I moved to the old mill, I brought Smoky Jack from Will's to live with me. Will had taken splendid care of the dog through the summer.

Every time Jean came to see us, she wanted to know when I was going to bring Smoky Jack to Knoxville. I wanted to keep him with me until Thanksgiving because there were a few scheduled hikes into the mountains when I could use him.

I was a fairly good carpenter so I found extra work between guiding trips. Smoky Jack seemed to adapt to this way of living. If I were helping build a new addition to the Mountain View Hotel, he was chained. If I worked for Marshall Ogle, a carpenter in his own right, the dog did not have to be chained and was allowed to go with me.

There had been some discussion among horse owners of Gatlinburg that a horseback trail to the top of Mount Le Conte was needed. Men living in the community who owned horses and rented them were all anxious to help put in a trail. They talked it over with their neighbors and decided the best route would be up Roaring Fork Creek, where there was already a road of sorts, to a spot above Sherman Clabo's home. From there the trail would go up to the Trillium Gap through dense forest and along the main connecting ridge between it and the top of Mount Le Conte. Will Ramsey and I thought a trail could be made from above Clabo's cabin to Trillium Gap without too much difficulty. It would entail hard work but, with a gang of men, all congenial and all working toward the same goal, we thought we could accomplish it.

Will and I were asked to be the "route" men since both of us knew the territory through which the trail would go. One day late in September, Smoky Jack and I walked up to Will's to ask him when we were going to start the trail. Will was not at home. His wife said he was working on the county road toward Greenbrier. I walked on up the road. I had gone about a mile, with Jack tagging along, when we came to a group of twelve or fifteen men working on the road with mattocks, shovels, picks, and brier hooks.

The foreman of the crew asked, "Paul, when are you going to put in your county road work?" This question took me by surprise. I told him I considered myself a citizen of Knoxville. I paid my poll tax[41] there and voted there.

---

41. During the early years of the twentieth century, payment of a poll tax was required before an individual could vote in Tennessee and many other states. The tacit intent of the tax was to keep poor people and minorities from voting. The poll tax provision in Tennessee was repealed in 1953.

He said, "No, you are a citizen of Sevier County now. You have lived in this county for more than a year and are subject to the laws governing the county. You either have to work the county roads for a week at this time of year or you will have to pay your road tax. Now, I am just as much interested in the horse trail to the top of Mount Le Conte as you are. Suppose you help us here for the remainder of the day and then tomorrow we will all go up into the woods and start the trail."

I could not question his way of putting things. I was anxious to get the trail started, so I worked on the road along with the others. When lunchtime came, the foreman and his laborers shared their lunches with me. Since it was Friday, we decided to wait until Monday before starting the horseback trail. I had a field notebook with me and made notes on what tools, foods, and other camping paraphernalia each man should bring. We decided to take a large tent with us and establish a camp above Clabo's cabin.

Four of us would take turns cooking. After breakfast, men would start work where they had left off the evening before. The cook would wash the dishes, prepare the noon lunches, and then walk up and work on the trail. We all chipped in money to buy the provisions we could not bring from our homes. None of us had too much to spend, but it was in the interest of all to help get that trail built.

I had written to the Champion Fibre Company and had received permission to construct a horseback trail to the top of the mountain. We had also received permission from Sherman Clabo to use his private sled road above his home and go through his part of Black Spruce Flats (Clabo's Woods). We had our right-of-way.

The following Monday morning, a few of us went to the store and bought food before meeting the others up the Roaring Fork Creek near Cliff Branch. We had two packhorses along to carry the tent, blankets, and other supplies. We made a base camp at the end of the sled road near Roaring Fork Creek. After setting up the camp, cutting a tree and splitting part of it to make an improvised eating table and benches, erecting our tent and ditching it, we still had a little time on our hands to work on the trail.

We thought it would be best to follow along Roaring Fork Creek for half a mile or so then make a switchback around a steep area and strike Surry Fork. We would work our way up for some distance, make a switchback or two up this stream, and go into the more open woods below Trillium Gap. For more than a mile, work was painfully slow. We had to cut our way through dense growths of rhododendron. Great horned and barred owls could be heard calling in the denseness of the woods.

There was a lot of mattock work to be done through the rhododendron thickets. The roots of the shrubs had to be taken out completely and small rocks and dirt had to be shoveled into those parts of the trail. To allow the trail to drain on hillsides, we half-buried a six- or seven-inch log diagonally across from the ditchline to let water drain off without washing out the trail. We did not work by any time clocks or take any coffee breaks. Each morning, when we arrived at the spot where we had stopped work the evening before, we set to work and cut trail until noon then gathered near a stream to eat our lunches. Then it was back to work. We would quit about sunset and walk back down to our base camp. The cook for the day would have already gone ahead to start supper for the group.

Many men worked on this trail, all volunteers. Will and I had to stay ahead of the group and scout to find the most convenient trail for a walking horse. We knew the area and had hunted and fished there. As the crew slowly worked up the sides of ridges toward Trillium Gap, we always managed to leave behind us broken branches and hacked places on trees for them to follow. When we had looked over the course thoroughly and were ahead of the crew half a mile or more, we would return and help in the construction of the trail, using shovels, mattocks, picks, axes, crosscut saws, machetes, and bolo knives. Will and I always carried bolo knives with us in our scouting and we took them with us as we worked our way upward. The other tools were always stacked near the end of the trail when we stopped work in the evenings. We wrapped the blades of our saws each night in oilcloth and hung them from a tree branch.

Smoky Jack went along. In the daytime he would play around in the woods. When we heard him bark, we would find he had caught gray squirrels. There would be fresh meat in camp that night. Smoky Jack caught groundhogs twice. We added these to our meals.

Most of the group in camp were farmers and needed to go home after work. They would leave their tools with us and promised to return as soon as possible. Different men and grown boys came in to help us, each of us working beside the others. We joked and kidded and had fun.

When men came into camp to spend a couple or more days with us, they brought along food from their home—fresh eggs, half a ham, bacon, live chickens, potatoes, cabbage, beans, and other garden vegetables. A few of us would eat their food, but there were always some who would not. That left more for those of us who relished the fresh groceries.

During the second week, I had to leave the trail work to guide a small group from Memphis to the top of Mount Le Conte. Jack Huff, then living by himself on top of the mountain, wanted to know how the work was progressing on the trail. I told him that, when I left the group after noon the previous day, the trail was within half a mile of Trillium Gap. This trail meant as much to Jack Huff as it meant for those renting horses. We had a discussion that night at the Basin Spring camp as to how we were going to get around that high bluff about halfway between Trillium Gap and the top of Mount Le Conte. I admitted that I did not know. We had not scouted that portion of the trail. We would work out our problems when we arrived there.

When I walked into our temporary camp on Monday morning, I found the cook almost ready to carry lunches up to the working crew. I stopped and helped him. I had brought food from the store and part of these provisions had been placed in Smoky Jack's saddle pockets. I carried the bulkier things in one of my pack baskets. Will's wife had seen me coming and called to me. Will had forgotten to take along a sack of frying apples. Would I take them with me? Sure. There was about a peck of them.

I helped the cook, Ed Ogle, carry the food on up to the crew. We found them working just below Trillium Gap. Will was working with the others. I kidded him a little about leaving a part of his provisions at home. He admitted that he had forgotten them but then said, "I knew that you would be along this morning and decided that you and Smoky

Jack wouldn't be loaded. I left them on purpose so you could bring them." The laugh was on me.

We ate our lunches in Trillium Gap. The elevation of Trillium Gap is 4,717 feet above sea level. We had made a trail up the ridge through dense woodland, rising more than 2,000 feet within two miles. We still had 2,000 feet to climb. We all knew that constructing the trail on top of the ridge would be much easier.

The next day, it was my turn to cook. I was up early, started a fire, and heated a kettle of water for coffee. I fixed apples for frying. After slicing them, I put lots of butter into a skillet and added the apples. I pulled out a small sack labeled SUGAR, and, after the apples had simmered for a while, I sprinkled several tablespoons of sugar on them. They did not look just right to me, but I did not taste them. I was busy cooking other food.

As the sun came up, men got up, went to the creek and washed, then came back into camp and drank cups of coffee to warm themselves. The fried apples were served with scrambled eggs, bacon, ponebread, hot oatmeal, and gravy.

Will was the first to take a big bite of those fried apples, hot from the skillet. His face turned all sorts of colors. He jumped up, spit the apples out, and took a large gulp of water. Turning to me, he cried, "Cook! Try those apples! They have been salted instead of sugared." I tasted them. Sure enough, I had used salt. I could not believe it! I got up from the table and went over to inspect the sack from which the seasoning had come. Sugar was plainly written on the sack. I brought it over to the table and let everyone else look at it. The apples were thrown into the garbage pit.

We made good progress that day working above the Gap. When we were within a quarter of a mile of the bluff, we ran into difficulty. We could not cut a trail for the horses up the bluff nor could we blast a trail. We scouted the area and decided among ourselves that this would be the end of the horse trail. Just below the bluff, there was a fairly large level place. We decided the best thing to do was to let the horses come this far and make a foot trail to the top of the mountain. The trail we made went directly to the East Peak, now known as Hightop, where it ran into the trail between there and Myrtle Point. After two more days of trail clearing, we spent the night with Jack Huff at the Basin Spring camp. The following day we returned to base camp, struck our tent, and returned to our homes.

Many horseback trips were made along the trail by those who wanted to ride that far and walk up the last thousand feet. We always took an extra man along to keep the horses under control and safe from bears. It was a delightful ride up this trail, although we were not able to complete it. Later, after the Great Smoky Mountains National Park was established, the Civilian Conservation[42] boys and men changed the trail and lengthened it by at least two miles.

I had practically promised my sister I would bring Smoky Jack into Knoxville about Thanksgiving to spend the winter with her and my mother. As Thanksgiving approached, I knew that I wanted to climb Mount Le Conte with Jack at least one more time.

One clear morning I walked up to the store to find out if Jack Huff had ordered supplies, thinking that Smoky Jack and I could take them that afternoon. There was a light order. I loaded Jack's saddle pockets and one of my pack baskets then walked back to the hotel to eat lunch before our climb. I chained Smoky Jack to one of the fence posts in the parking area, walked on up on the porch, and announced that the dog and I would be hiking to the top of the mountain after lunch.

Mrs. Huff introduced me to some of her friends from Virginia. One of the women wanted a picture of Smoky Jack and me. I did not like the idea and tried to slip away unnoticed. The woman followed me into the road and took two pictures of us together. I forgot about posing for the pictures until I received copies in the mail. One of them was used in my first book, *Mt. LeConte* (published in 1966).

---

42. Civilian Conservation Corps (CCC) was instituted as part of the New Deal with the goal of conserving natural resources by employing young men to work during the economic downturn of the Great Depression. Many of the trails, bridges, and buildings in the Great Smoky Mountains National Park were built by the Civilian Conservation Corpsmen. There were twenty-two CCC camps in the Great Smoky Mountains National Park.

Smoky Jack and I were happy as we made our climb over the new horseback trail to the top of Mount Le Conte. We arrived before dark. Jack Huff was glad to see us. He had been by himself several days and was lonesome.

We spent three days with him and helped about the camp to pay for our board. One night, we sat beside his battery-powered radio and listened to every station we could pick up, getting their call numbers and letters. The stations totaled nearly one hundred.

We talked of the future development of the camp, of guide work, and of the possibility of re-entering school in the spring quarter. We talked of work during the winter. He told me he did not believe he would stay on the mountain that winter as I had done the previous year, but he would probably come down and work in one of his father's sawmills until spring came.

Smoky Jack went exploring in the woods and had his little runs by himself. Once he was chased by a stray timber wolf. The dog seemed to be right at home and enjoyed every minute. His old kennel was still there and at night he slept in it.

I told Jack Huff that the main reason we had come this time to the top of the mountain was because I was taking Smoky Jack into Knoxville to live with my sister and mother for the winter. I did not wish to get rid of him, but my mother and Jean wanted him to spend one winter with them. I think this was the last time I saw Jack Huff on the mountain by himself.

It was hard for Jack and me to tear ourselves away. I felt we were at the end of an era in our lives together and I did not want it to end. The woods and distant views were beautiful that afternoon as we made our way slowly down the mountain.

I paused every now and then to listen to the birds. I stopped to look at the distant landscape. We walked from Trillium Gap out to Brushy to see the beautiful view from there, then retraced our steps into the gap and slowly came on down toward Gatlinburg. It was dark before we reached the old mill and the night was very cool.

Each time a person changes his residence he makes new friends and acquaintances. Smoky Jack had four Tennessee homes after I bought him. He lived with me on top of Mount Le Conte as my companion. In 1926, before Thanksgiving, he took up residence at my parents' home in Knoxville and remained there for over a year. He moved with the family to Alpine, Tennessee, in 1928, when my father took a pastorate there. He then came to Crab Orchard in 1935 to live his remaining days with my wife, Maxine, and me.

During his Knoxville days, Jack became a companion to my mother and sister. He became a family dog. He was content to stay in the neighborhood and spend most of his time in our yard. He had accepted Jean and Mother's handling of him, and I think he looked forward to their evening excursions. Often he accompanied them to the neighborhood store without being chained.

Each time I returned to my parents' home, he was my constant companion and followed me everywhere. Our hiking forays into the Great Smokies were becoming less and less frequent since most of my work from 1927 until 1929 was in northern states. Then I spent another two years in and around Knoxville before again working in the North. In 1933, health forced me to return to the South from then on, for the rest of Jack's life. I never worked again in the North.

Jack knew when I was preparing to leave home. For twenty-four hours before my departure, he would hardly let me out of his sight. He always wanted to sleep on a rug beside my bed and he would be the last one I would bid goodbye. He would have to be shut up in the house for an hour or so after my departure to prevent his trying to follow me.

I came home in 1928 and helped my parents move from Knoxville to Alpine, on the middle level of the Cumberland Plateau. I remained there for several weeks after the move. Jack and I learned much about that area together and when I went hiking he went along with me. We had many happy times together. Once in a great while, I took him back to Knoxville so he could accompany me up Mount Le Conte again. He seemed to enjoy these outings but, when he became ten years old, I stopped his wearing saddle pockets.

In Alpine, Jack made many friends. He confined his activities to the Presbyterian manse's grounds and to nearby Alpine Institute's[43] campus of several hundred acres. He did not take to wandering nor would he take up with packs of dogs and roam over the countryside. Soon after the family moved to Alpine, he had to whip every dog in the neighborhood and let them know who was boss. But he never took up with a running pack. Most dogs in the neighborhood left the immediate campus and parsonage grounds alone and would not venture on them. The exception was that sometimes packs of hounds would drive a fox across our yard at night. But Jack would not go out to attack the hounds. He would come out of his large kennel to watch the hounds as they passed through our yard when chasing the fox and then he would return to his bed for the rest of the night.

Resident teachers at the school all knew Smoky Jack and he was friendly with most of them. He was particularly fond of Mrs. Flora Jones, matron of the girls' dormitory, who took care of him during winter months when my father had to leave to raise money in northern states for the Home Missionary Department of the Presbyterian Church. Mother sometimes would go to her mother's home in Toledo, Ohio. During such times, some teacher would take up residence in the manse while my parents were gone. Smoky Jack went to live in the girls' dormitory where Mrs. Jones took care of him. They liked each other and he would accompany her on walks in the immediate area.

Smoky Jack was known on campus as "Jack Adams." He was rarely referred to by his real name. I think that the dormitory students of the school gave him that name, for he had many friends among them. There were a few of the boys who stayed there in the summer when school

---

43. Alpine Institute was a Presbyterian school located in Alpine (Overton County), Tennessee. In 1928, Adams moved to Alpine with his family after his father accepted a pastorate there.

was not in session to work on the school's farm, milk the cows, do repair work, paint, and operate the school's electrical plant, thus helping themselves obtain an education.

Two of Smoky Jack's pups were raised by me in the course of his life. The last one, born in 1933, was to become "the ears" for Smoky Jack in his later years. Jean named this pup Nicodemus, but we called him Nick most of the time. He had a habit of tantalizing the older dog and would make life miserable for him sometimes. Jack tolerated his offspring, but he did not like to play the part of a mother, too. So, after taking much unwanted play and teasing from the pup, he would slip off and disappear on the campus for the rest of the day then come home about suppertime.

Once in a while I wanted to go hunting or take a long walk up the side of Alpine Mountain so Jack could try to teach his young son something about hunting. The three of us walked up the side of the mountain. The pup would always want to play with his father. I had to carry a chain along with me in order to control the younger dog while Jack hunted. After several of these experiences, the younger dog learned that he, too, was supposed to hunt. He forgot about play at these times. I do not think Jack ever lost his sense of smell. Sometimes when they were trailing an animal and the younger dog barked, Jack would turn around and grab the younger dog by the shoulder gently and shake him a little. Jack wanted the younger dog to keep quiet until the animal was treed.

By the time Nick was a year old, he had outgrown most of his puppyhood traits and the two dogs got along a great deal better. I had taught Nick several of the commands which Smoky Jack obeyed readily. He obeyed them, too. Nick never learned how to follow Jack when he went over on the campus. He never acquired the sense of smell which was so keen in Jack. Jack was beginning to lose his hearing and, as time went on, he became deaf. We had to raise our voices to speak to him. The younger dog became his father's ears and Jack would keep an eye on Nick and know by his actions what was going on.

I have seen Jack punish his pups many times. One incident stands out in my mind. Sometimes a pup would get into the screened-in back porch or he would find a shoe, slipper, or overshoe and proceed to take it into the back yard and chew on it. Whenever Jack found one of them doing this, he would walk over to the pup and growl quietly at him, pick him up by the nape of the neck, and shake the pup gently before dropping his offspring. Then, still growling, Jack would pick up the footwear and carry it to the door of the porch, bark a time or two to be let in, and deposit the shoe beside its mate. Then he would open the screen door by himself and go on about his business.

Smoky Jack had some complexities which I never fully understood. Whether he learned these traits in police school or not, I do not know. The man through whom I purchased the dog had told me a great many of the commands which the dog knew, but I do not think that he himself knew all that had been taught the dog. From time to time I learned more about him.

There were two young men on campus with whom the dog would go when I was not at home. He could be persuaded to go with them easily, for he liked both of them. One was Ralph Hall of the Big Lick Community of Cumberland County, who for two consecutive summers remained to work at the school. Whenever Ralph would whistle for Smoky Jack from the opposite side of the baseball diamond near the manse, the dog would respond and go to him, provided there was not much of interest going on around the house. They would accompany each other from place to place. Jack would return by suppertime.

I came home very unexpectedly one time during the school term and Jack was not around to greet me. Mother informed me that he had gone with Ralph that morning and would probably not show up until evening. After I had been home for a little while, I went walking over the campus to find Jack. The school principal whom I met thought that I would find Ralph and some of the boys in a field above the campus, grubbing stumps from newly cleared ground. I went in that direction. I passed through two gates and soon entered a new field. I found a group of boys. Some were throwing small burning objects upon the ground along with cigarettes, which they were not allowed to smoke on campus. Jack was putting them out. These boys had been watching him put out the smoking objects and were making great sport of it. Ralph, who was supposed to be their leader, was not with them.

When I lived on Mount Le Conte, I smoked cigarettes and cigars but was always careful to snub them out once I had finished with them. Whether my dog approved of my tobacco habit, I do not know. But he would watch me as I snubbed them with my foot upon the ground to be sure that they were out. Many smokers did not attempt to extinguish butts when they were finished but merely flipped them out of their hands to the ground. Whenever this happened and the dog was in their presence, he would walk over to the still-smoking object and with his nose pile dirt upon it. If by that time it was not extinguished, he would sort of prance with both front feet upon the little pile of nosed-up dirt, both front feet striking the pile together, and not be willing to go on until he was satisfied that the last spark was extinguished. Many hikers had seen him do this.

During Smoky Jack's early days and until he was about eight or nine years old, he was a very swift runner and a good high-jumper. I have seen him clear many nine-foot fences with ease and I have seen him jump as high as twelve feet up the trunk of a tree while in pursuit of a squirrel. As he grew older, he lost his speed and sometimes misjudged the height of a fence or other object over which he wanted to jump. He also knew how to climb a ladder which was pitched not more than sixty degrees.

He would sometimes chase rabbits. The rabbit, when pursued too closely, would stop abruptly and squat down in front of the dog. Jack, as large and heavy as he was, would run past it some distance and then sheepishly return to my side as if embarrassed. The rabbit, of course, had made his getaway.

A number of schools probably have farms and pastures connected with them where crops are raised for the school's boarding students. Alpine Institute had such a farm. One day Mother asked me to take something to the school dispensary on my way up Alpine Mountain. After I had made the delivery, I recalled tales about a Jersey bull quartered in a large pasture to the rear of the dispensary. Not wanting to walk half a mile around it, I decided that I would go through it, accompanied by Jack. As we walked over a little knoll in the pasture, I saw the bull. He saw us, too, and lowered his head to charge. Jack saw the bull about the same time and stood his ground, ears alert, snarling. As the bull started charging toward me, I gave Jack the "attack" command. He leaped into action, running toward the bull and sinking his teeth into his nostrils and hanging on. The bull tried to throw off the dog but with no success. Then the bull went to his knees and finally straightened out prostrate on the ground. The struggle was over. I commanded the dog to release his hold. As he did so, the bull quickly got up and lumbered to one corner of the pasture where it stood and watched us pass through. Never again did that bull fail to retreat to the pasture corner where a few trees had been left for shade. He had had enough of that large black dog!

It was now safe for anyone accompanied by the dog to cross the pasture. Even Mrs. Jones, with Smoky Jack at her side, could walk across the pasture instead of going around it. It was a short cut for her to a favorite trail up the mountain.

One day a teacher at the school called on the phone. He told me that Smoky Jack was hung up in a barbed-wire fence and would not allow anyone to get him out. I hung up the receiver and made a dash for the garage. I knew that the car would get me there quicker than I could run or walk. Grabbing a pair of heavy wire cutters, I drove to the driveway between the Laurels and the school dispensary.

Smoky Jack was caught with one of his rear feet between the two top wires of the fence. His front feet could barely touch the ground, then only one at a time. He was under a severe strain. He was growling fiercely and would not allow anyone in the crowd which had gathered to approach him.

As I walked up, he quieted down and wagged his tail. The fence was a little over seven feet high. Handing my pliers to a student, I asked him to cut the lower wire as I tried to lift the dog up by running my hands in under his body. I knew that he would not bite me. I had helped him when he had previously been caught in a large steel trap. When I lifted the dog, the student cut the wire. A teacher reached over gingerly and pushed the dog's rear leg over the top wire and I set Jack down upon the ground. I examined him closely for possible broken bones. I could not find any broken bones, but he did limp as we went back to the car. When we got out of the car at the manse, Jack did not limp. He seemed to be normal, but I knew that he had a few strained muscles, for he had been hanging in that fence for more than half an hour.

One Sunday morning, I noticed a long line of smoke rising from the east side of Alpine Mountain. I walked over to the campus and tried to find someone to go with me to the top of the mountain to help fight the fire. All of the dormitory boys were gone. Smoky Jack and I ascended the mountain by walking from the manse property.

I had to return home about noon that day to take Father to two of his outstations, but I told Mr. Burr and John Vaughn, owners of the property where the fire was raging, that if they did not have it out by the time I came back with Father, I would return and continue to help fight it. On our way to Father's outstations, he told me that he did not have enough men in church that morning to take up the collection. He had called upon some of the female teachers to substitute for the men. All men of the community were on the fire line, including the dormitory boys, the principal of the school, and the male teachers.

When we returned home about nine o'clock that night, red haze could be seen beyond the mountain top, a sign that the fire was still raging. I called the principal to inquire if there was anyone around who would accompany Smoky Jack and me to help the men already on the spot. He told me that he and the boys had been on the fire line all day. Because they had to go to school the next day, he had called a halt to their efforts and all of them had returned to the school. I called Mrs. Vaughn and asked her if her menfolk had come down for food and coffee. Receiving a negative reply, I promised her that, if she would have something ready for them within an hour, I would come by and get it. After our conversation she must have called neighbors whose men were up there on the fire line. When Smoky Jack and I arrived at her home, there were two big, heaping baskets of food ready to go up to the firefighters.

It was a considerably shorter distance for me to drive to the Vaughns' and walk up the mountain than to go directly from Alpine. I packed Smoky Jack's saddle pockets with canteens and a first-aid kit, thinking perhaps there might be a few burned men up on the mountain. It was two and a half miles to the Vaughns' and just a half-mile by trail past a fine spring to the top of the mountain. Jack and I could make better time going that way.

When I strapped Jack's saddle pockets on him at the Vaughns,' the wives of the men fighting the fire all stood around in disbelief. I do not believe any of them had ever seen Smoky Jack with his saddle pockets on, although they had heard of him being packed this way. I placed some food in the saddle pockets and tied a stout rope to two one-gallon bottles to swing across my shoulders. I told the women as I picked up the baskets that I would fill the bottles and canteens with water at the spring before topping out on the mountain.

Smoky Jack and I hiked up the mountain. At the spring I filled the empty canteens and bottles with water, for I figured these fellows were thirsty as well as hungry. Because I believed that the men were fighting the fire to our east, we walked out an old trail in that direction. The dog and I had gone about half a mile before we met two firefighters who had started down the mountain by the same trail to obtain food and water. The two were very surprised to see us coming with two big baskets of food.

We walked back to where the others were still fighting the fire. One elderly man spoke as the dog and I walked up to him and said, "Why Paul, we never expected you to come back up here."

I replied, "Well, I called up your wife and she told me that none of you had been down or sent down for food. I'd promised to come back, and here I am."

"Let's all get together and go over on the west side of the mountain to eat and drink, then we'll get back on the fire line."

We did. By dawn, we had the fire extinguished. As we raked leaves and brush away from the lane we were trying to put around the fire—so it would not cross to the western side of the mountain—Smoky Jack stayed close. After the fire was out, one of the men and I walked along its perimeter to be sure that it had not jumped the lane. We all left the mountaintop about the same time. I was asked to stay at the Vaughns' for a hearty breakfast.

Later, about five o'clock, I noticed smoke rising again from near the top of the mountain. Did we have a firebug? I scarcely knew what to do. I called the Vaughns and told them that I could see smoke rising from the west side of the mountain. Could they? There was a high knob between them and the top of the mountain, so they could not see any smoke. I told them that I was coming up to help put out this second fire. The Vaughns phoned others and, by the time I drove up to their house with Jack, there had gathered quite a group of men who had started up the mountain to help put out the fire. We worked for an hour before extinguishing it. This fire was in a different location and not at all near the burned-over area where many of these same men had helped fight a fire fewer than twelve hours earlier.

Discussing this on our way back down the mountain, some of us decided that there must be a firebug in the vicinity. The next afternoon before school was out, I took Smoky Jack in a circular direction to the top of Alpine Mountain. I had already suspected where the next fire would be started, if the firebug maintained a pattern.

Jack and I were standing near the trail in the unburnt part of the woods an hour after school had dismissed for the day. The dog gave off a low growl and pointed down toward the foot of the mountain. His ruff rose as he stood at attention. He had heard something or someone. I looked in the direction he pointed and saw a young man walking up the trail, a youngster whom my parents had been helping financially through school. He lived a mile or so from where we spied him.

Looking all around, he knelt to the ground and lit a match and applied it to dry leaves and grass. Fire started at once. He walked about twenty-five feet and repeated the same process to start another fire. He rose again and came a little closer to us. He had just knelt when I called to him, saying, "Don't do that!" Startled, he started running in the opposite direction. I called to him, "Stop, or I will hiss Smoky Jack on you!" He knew Smoky Jack and he knew that if the dog attacked he could not possibly get to his home or anyplace else before the dog would overtake him. He stopped short in his tracks.

I walked up to him and said, "Let's get brush and put these fires out."

He asked, "What are you going to do, Mr. Adams?" I told him that he could consider himself under arrest for the moment. I was in a quandary over what to do. I had arrested a man. I was a state conservation officer and I had a duty to perform. But, if this young man did not show up at his home in a limited amount of time, his parents would become worried.

The closest way to his home from the spot where I arrested him was about a mile and a half from the Vaughns' on whose property we stood. I had not driven to the Vaughns'. I had walked from the manse to the top of the mountain. But I knew that John Vaughn would drive us into Livingston where this young man could be placed in jail and warrants made out against him. I ordered the boy to start walking toward the Vaughn home. He pleaded with me to forget the whole incident, but I told him that I was going to place him in jail for safekeeping. As we started down the mountain, I had him walk ahead. I told Smoky Jack to "heel." I did not have any handcuffs, although I was armed. We arrived at the farmhouse in about twenty-five minutes.

I told John Vaughn what I had seen, saying that I had arrested the boy. John said, "I'll take you and him right on in to Livingston, if you say so." I answered, "Let's go."

We drove the twelve miles to Livingston and lodged the young man in the Overton County jail, although he repeatedly begged me to let him off. I did not know whether the men of the Alpine community would want to prosecute this boy or not, but I thought that one night in jail might work wonders on his mind. The jailer, who happened to be his uncle, talked to him after John, Smoky Jack, and I had left.

Because of his absence from home, the boy's father had gone looking for him. He had walked down to the school and inquired from the boy's teachers and school principal whether his son had been kept after school. They told him that he was dismissed from school at the same time as the other students. The father went over to the manse, suspecting he might be working there. Father told this man that I had gone to the top of Alpine Mountain with Smoky Jack to try to catch a firebug and that I had not as yet returned.

When John Vaughn let Smoky Jack and me out of his car at home, we were met by the boy's father. He was distraught when I told him that I had caught his son setting the woods on fire on top of Alpine Mountain. He wanted my permission to go into Livingston and get the boy. I said,

"No, we can't do that. I think that a night in jail might do the boy some good." The father said that, if I would release the boy to him, he would take him home and give him the thrashing of his life. To this I could not agree. I knew that this man had a reputation as a high-tempered individual who believed in harsh punishment. He frequently gave his children "thrashings" and they bore the marks of his beatings for days afterwards.

When the boy's father had left for his home, John Vaughn called and asked me to meet with a group of men at his home the next morning, preparatory to going to Livingston. He reminded me that there was much ugly sentiment around. I knew that this boy, under eighteen years of age, would have to be tried by the county judge, who was very hard on juveniles brought before him.

The next morning, I drove up to John's and met those gathered there, including the boy's father. We decided among ourselves that we would not prosecute this boy, but we would give him a chance to make something of himself. We knew that the county judge would in all probability send the boy to a reform school, a place where none of us thought he belonged. We demanded of the father that he, in turn, would not thrash his son for his acts. He gave his promise.

John Vaughn, one of his older sons, the boy's father, and I then drove into Livingston to the jail. We talked to the boy. His uncle, who had given his nephew a good lecture the previous night, turned the boy over to his father after we had talked to him about his acts of destruction. He admitted that he had started the fire I had seen near the top of the mountain Monday evening but denied having started the one which swept up Medlock Hollow Sunday morning. I did not believe he had started it. His father was an honest man and told us that the boy was at home when this fire was started.

Today, this boy whom Smoky Jack and I caught setting fire to the woods works for the United States Forest Service. He looked me up several years ago and thanked me for giving him another chance at normal life.

Nicodemus, one of Smoky Jack's male pups, moved to Crab Orchard with me and my wife, Maxine, the first of April 1935. We moved into a small house on what we called "our five acres adjoining our larger acreage." Four of these five acres were cleared. We purchased both land parcels. This gave us a place to live on the five acres. We could start clearing land on the larger tract and build a permanent house later in the year. We had many plants to move from Alpine.[44]

The house on the five acres was not much of a house, but it would have to be our temporary home. It was set on rock and tree-trunk pillars with a basement under it. There was also a privy nearby. We carried our cooking and drinking water from a big spring across a hill on the larger parcel of land. The spring had furnished water for many generations. When we moved to Crab Orchard, there were several families who obtained their water from this spring. Our purchase of the land around it did not change their water supply.

Father and Mother did not leave Alpine to move into Knoxville for more than two months after Maxine and I moved to Crab Orchard. I had planned on bringing Smoky Jack and Nick with us because Mother did not want to be responsible for the older dog in Knoxville. But when I had suggested this to Mother, she quickly said, "No." She would keep Smoky Jack until they moved. We could take his pup with us, but Jack stayed. I consented to do it the way she wanted. She thought it would be a relief for Smoky Jack to be free of the younger dog for the time being. Mother liked Nick, as all of us did, but she knew the pup gave Jack a miserable life sometimes.

After we moved to Crab Orchard, Mother told me that Smoky Jack quit going over on the Alpine Institute campus. He was content to stay at the manse and keep an eye on Father and Mother. When we went to the manse, he followed us around as we dug and loaded plants which we had growing there before transporting them to Crab Orchard. Once our trailer was loaded, he wanted to come with us. He would somehow slip into the car or take a perch on the load of plants. When I would call him, he would not respond. Perhaps he knew I would take him into the

---

44. In 1934, Paul Adams and his wife, Maxine, established their nursery, Alpine Floral Gardens, in Alpine, Tennessee. When they later moved to Crab Orchard, they kept the original name of the nursery. The nursery specialized in native and bedding plants.

house and tell Mother or Father to keep an eye on him for an hour or so, or until Maxine and I were gone. Afterward, they told me, he would go out into the yard, smell the car tracks and the spot where I had last stood before getting into the car, take a sniff or two into the air, then go back to the stoop and lie down.

Maxine and I helped Father and Mother move back to Knoxville in June 1935, where they retired. We left Nick at our Crab Orchard home with a hired man. Smoky Jack knew, from all the commotion going on before Maxine and I arrived on the scene, that they were moving again. The movers from Knoxville were placing the last of two truckloads of household furniture on their vans when we arrived that morning. Neighbors had come to see the folks off.

Father and Mother were to drive my car. Smoky Jack and I were to drive the family car as far as Crab Orchard. I was then to drive my parents to Knoxville to their Kenyon Avenue home, returning to Crab Orchard that evening.

Smoky Jack seemed perfectly content as he rode beside me that morning. It must have seemed like old times, when he accompanied me on many collecting trips, to and from Knoxville and to other distant points while living in Alpine. He sat on his haunches and occasionally looked wistfully at me. I would put a hand on him to more or less comfort him. I was wondering how he, as an old dog, and Nick, after so lengthy a separation, would greet each other once we reached our destination, Crab Orchard.

Instead of driving down into the yard, we parked our cars on the side of the nearby highway. Nick had heard the two cars and came dashing up the hill to greet us. When I opened the door for Jack to get out, Nick immediately became arrogant, his ruff raised. He was ready to fight for supremacy over his home. The two dogs sniffed noses. The ruff on Smoky Jack never raised. He sidled up to me, seeming to ask, "Have I got to tolerate him again?"

Nick had whipped every dog in the vicinity of our new home and thought he was "king of the roost." But I noticed that his ruff suddenly went down. His arrogance disappeared and he became playful with his father.

Upon my return from Knoxville that night, Maxine told me that Nick had taken up his duties of "being the ears" for Smoky Jack and that the two dogs had been getting along fine, following her about in the small fenced-in area of our five acres.

As Maxine and I worked on the place, the two dogs roamed nearby. Frequently we would take both of them when traveling. Usually, when I returned to Alpine to dig and move more plants for our Crab Orchard gardens, I would take only Smoky Jack along, leaving Nick at home. A few times I took Smoky Jack into Knoxville with me.

When we would go after our mail at the local post office late each evening, we would allow both dogs to have the run of the yard. They knew that these trips would not be lengthy. We were in the habit of going together. I to get our mail, Maxine to buy a few groceries.

We had fenced in the five acres to keep roaming cattle and hogs out of our gardens. We had two wide gates on opposite sides of the fence so that the car could be driven to our house from Tennessee Highway 70. Each time we drove to and from our place, we had to open the gate and then fasten it after the car had passed through. We had trained Nick to follow only driveways and paths. Smoky Jack had his own short cuts. We allowed him this leeway because he was old. It was Smoky Jack who was allowed to enter the house at night and lie on the floor beside one of us until bedtime.

Smoky Jack was becoming deaf. In mid-1935, when we were in Knoxville, I called Dr. Jacobs and asked him if I could bring his old dog friend to his office for a complete physical. The doctor thought that was a good idea. Dog and doctor seemed pleased to see each other. But Jack did not have the old enthusiasm to jump and play around as he had in former years. Dr. Jacobs told me that there was nothing wrong with the dog except that he was getting old and perhaps would go blind. The doctor inquired how old he was and I informed him that Jack was past fourteen. The doctor shook his head as he told me it was possible for the dog to die at any time. He felt sure we had taken good care of him, for he had already lived to a ripe old age.

Smoky Jack would keep his eye on Nick and he would respond to Nick's movements. We could easily comprehend from Jack's actions that he was aging faster and faster. No more was there jumping or rearing up on his hind feet when we were about to take our walks. There was a definite stiffness in him. We noticed it. Yet, he was always eager to go along with us despite his infirmities.

The two dogs had their separate dishes where food was served to them. They had a common drinking pan in which they could always find water. It was near the entrance to our house.

One of the first things I built after we moved to Crab Orchard was a dog kennel. I built it large enough to take care of two full-grown German shepherd dogs. It was pretty roomy for Nick but I wondered, when Smoky Jack came to live with us, just what would happen when Jack moved into it. Would Nick allow his father to sleep on cedar chips in his doghouse? There was no argument there. That issue turned out the same as at the gate when Jack came to live with us. Jack was the dominant one who tolerated Nick beside him, the same as he had at Alpine. We noticed, however, that when someone passed our house at night, it was always Nick who barked the first time during the few weeks Smoky Jack lived here.

When we went for the mail and to the local store, the dogs remained at the house. Upon our return, they heard the sound of the car and came running up the hill to greet us. Nick followed the driveway. Smoky Jack made a short cut across a large bed of irises to welcome us home. Both dogs ran. Jack was usually the first to reach the gate.

One evening upon our return from the post office, Nick ran up the hill. Smoky Jack did not. We thought this strange, but Nick never indicated that anything was wrong. He never tried to lead us anywhere. After the car had been driven through the gate and the gate closed, he followed us to the house. I looked around outside for Smoky Jack, but I could not find him. I called loudly, thinking maybe Jack had wandered off, but received no response. I always had a fear that when it came Jack's time to die, he would go off by himself to do so and perhaps we would not find him for days.

At least, that was spared us. Looking toward the path which Smoky Jack always took to meet us at the gate, I saw his body lying prone on the far side of the little stream which ran down through the hollow. Dried mud was on his rear feet. In all probability, he had started out to meet us at the gate, had jumped the stream, and at that instant had died.

He was coming to meet us. What a natural way to be overtaken by death.

We buried Smoky Jack on our larger tract of land. I thought then that, after our business was well established on the larger tract, we might want to dispose of the smaller tract. I wanted him to lie near our future home. One of our local workers who loved Jack carved a tombstone for him. We placed this at the head of his grave. There have been but few times since we laid him to rest that one of us, sometimes both of us, have not picked up a rock or pebble and laid it on his grave as we passed by.

That ever-growing pile of stones on his grave is a landmark that always brings wonderful memories of a man's best friend.

CUMBERLAND JACK II OF EDELWEIS (ALSO KNOWN AS SMOKY JACK) GRAVE STONE. PAUL J. ADAMS PHOTOGRAPH COLLECTION. UNIVERSITY OF TENNESSEE, KNOXVILLE LIBRARIES.

SELECTED BIBLIOGRAPHY

Manuscripts

Great Smoky Mountains Conservation Papers, Great Smoky Mountains
National Park Archives.

Ilene Jones Cornwell Papers, MS 2054. University of Tennessee, Knoxville
Libraries.

Paul Jay Adams (1901–1985) Papers, 1918–1962; Paul Jay Adams (1901–1985)
Papers, Addition I, 1912–1977. Tennessee State Library and Archives.

Books and Databases

Ancestry.com. Census records, Tennessee Birth and Death records, and other
public records from 1920–1940.

Cain, Stanley A., and L. R. Hesler. "Harry Milliken Jennison, 1885–1940."
Journal of the Tennessee Academy of Science 15, no, 2 (April 1940): 173–76.

Campbell, Carlos. *Birth of a National Park in the Great Smoky Mountains.*
Knoxville: University of Tennessee Press, 1960.

Duncan, Thomas J. *The Golden Years of the Smoky Mountains Hiking Club,
1924–1974.* Knoxville: The Smoky Mountains Hiking Club, 1976.

Greve, Jeanette S. *The Story of Gatlinburg.* Strasburg, VA: Shenandoah
Publishing House, 1931.

Maddox, Marie. *A Lifetime in Gatlinburg: Martha Cole Whaley Remembers.*
Charleston: History Press, 2014.

Pierce, Daniel S. *The Great Smokies: From Natural Habitat to National Park.*
Knoxville: University of Tennessee Press, 2000.

Temple, Kenton, and Karen McDonald. *Gatlinburg.* Charleston: Arcadia
Publishing, 2011.

Wise, Kenneth, and Ron Petersen. *A Natural History of Mount Le Conte.*
Knoxville: University of Tennessee Press, 1998.